Walking Light

To M + D,
With much love and
deep thanks for all
you have given me;
most especially, the
need to be crucially
spoken to.

Love
Kibby

July 4 2001

STEPHEN DUNN

Walking Light

MEMOIRS AND ESSAYS ON POETRY

New Expanded Edition

American Readers Series, No. 4

BOA EDITIONS, LTD. ✦ ROCHESTER, NEW YORK ✦ 2001

First Edition
00 01 02 03 7 6 5 4 3 2 1

Publications by BOA Editions, Ltd. — a not-for-profit corporation under section
501 (c) (3) of the United States Internal Revenue Code — are made possible with
the assistance of grants from the Literature Program of the New York State Coun-
cil on the Arts, the Literature Program of the National Endowment for the Arts, the
Sonia Raiziss Giop Charitable Foundation, The Halcyon Hill Foundation, The
Chase Manhattan Foundation, as well as from the Mary S. Mulligan Charitable
Trust, the County of Monroe, NY, and The CIRE Foundation. See page 104 for
special individual acknowledgments.

Cover Design: Lisa Mauro / Mauro Design
Art: *Pure Interval* (oil on paper) by Steve Carpenter, courtesy of the author
Interior design and composition: Valerie Brewster, Scribe Typography
Manufacturing: McNaughton & Gunn, Lithographers
BOA Logo: Mirko

LIBRARY OF CONGRESS CATALOGING-IN-PUBLICATION DATA

Dunn, Stephen, 1939–
    Walking light: memoirs and essays on poetry / by Stephen Dunn. – New and
    expanded ed.
        p. cm. – (American readers series; no. 4)
    ISBN 1-929918-00-3 (alk. paper)
        1. Dunn, Stephen, 1939– 2. Poets, American – 20th century – Biography.
    3. Poetry – Authorship. I. Title. II. Series

    PS3554.U49 W34 2001
    811'.54 – DC21   00-140136
    [B]

BOA Editions, Ltd.
Steven Huff, Publisher
Richard Garth, Chair, Board of Directors
A. Poulin, Jr., President & Founder (1976–1996)
260 East Avenue
Rochester, NY 14604

www.boaeditions.org

NATIONAL
ENDOWMENT
FOR THE ARTS

State of the Arts

NYSCA

For Carol Houck Smith

CONTENTS

Walking Light

At the Crossroads:
An Introduction

PAUL VALERY FAMOUSLY LIKENED POETRY TO DANCING, PROSE TO walking. I suspect that about each he was half right. Nevertheless, we are the choreographers of our poems. We intuit, will, pace, digress, suppress, stitch, and arrange – all of which requires a sense of evolving design, and, finally, of a form that best serves what ultimately we've found ourselves to be doing.

A free verse poem (one of my chief concerns here) is a dance made of words, which moves at a rate not dictated by any theory, a dance on an open road. That road is often crooked, various small paths intersect it, and it's no doubt full of psychic debris; as we traverse it we're carrying the baggage of a life-lived and of a book-life, the entire history of our reading. So much wants to get into the poem!

Suppression of unnecessary impulses civilizes the poem, allows its various parts to better cohabit. At best, such suppression – by eliminating the false freedoms of indulgence and solipsism – makes freedom more possible. At worst, it leads to a kind of benignity, the poem so civilized that we'd like to mess up its hair, take it for a joy ride. It is the imagination's task to accommodate unruly impulses, to eventually make them feel inevitable. Poems should shimmer with a necessity, or otherwise be "holidays of the mind" – romps for the serious, trips to worlds that resemble ours. On the open road, how can we not look in many directions, take little side journeys? How can we not move – as circumstance dictates – gracefully sometimes, more hesitantly others? Finally, we don't know what an unnecessary impulse is until the poem has found its destination.

If we know about the "why" of a poem from the outset, we might not let intuition and imagination compete with our intentions and their rational inclinations. The mix, ideally, produces a kind of vitality, a vitality in search of a form that will be its no-nonsense legislator. Form solidifies design. It fixes the rational and the para-rational into a perpetual fluidity.

Along the way there will be crossroads where drifts and counterdrifts make their claims. Where to go next? At what pace to get there? Sometimes the dilemma is obviated by the speed we've picked up because we've been propelled from discovery to discovery, the labors of conscious choosing happily transcended. Or sometimes drift and counterdrift is the very modus operandi of the poem, its next moment found by refining and/or resisting what preceded it: a dance of contraries, its tempo dependent on the exigencies of the moment. Often the sounds of words will seek companionable sounds, and help lead us in the right direction. For that to happen we probably need to have been on one of the many right roads available to us. A right road, not surprisingly, tends to find other right roads.

If, for whatever reasons, we are on a wrong road, we must stop entirely, or know we must double back, or even trust that going blindly ahead and getting lost might be a way to find ourselves in new, more fruitful territory. Or we might need to be sly enough, like Frost, to construct a fiction about choosing a road less traveled — travel as metaphor for personal growth mocked and thrown into question. Though it has become commonplace these days to write the poem about writing the poem that we're writing, such a poem points to another way of making decisions at crossroads: to solve the problem of *what next* by adopting a different principle of selection.

But long, ponderous thinking usually gets us nowhere. If in our uncertainties we then resort to a map — say, some famous model insufficiently departed from — it could be the equivalent of placing ourselves on somebody else's best road, fine for the apprentice, but not for the poet who wishes to distinguish himself or herself.

Nevertheless, the history of poetry needs always to be behind us, like a parent who simultaneously shows the way and, for our own good, cautions against divergences, whose house we must honor and finally leave. A poet is someone who is constantly liberated and constricted.

Young poets who don't think of themselves as apprentices are notorious for resisting influences. They've only experienced the first stages of that limiting self-consciousness that comes with knowledge. They don't want anything to stop them from thinking that what they've done is original. Originality, of course, is what occurs when something new arises out of what's already been done. Poets who remain poets have, presumably, worked through the terrors of influence, and are willing to acknowledge their debts by using them in order to go their own way. They've learned what Thomas Mann knew: "A writer is somebody for whom writing is more difficult than it is for other people."

It's when the journey is over that a different kind of fun and travail begins. The revision process is when we worry the poem toward its virtues. We arrange and rearrange, suppress and add. We try to make it seem as if we danced all the way home.

What follows are various extensions of the above, explorations of the poetic process and of poems chosen to be illustrative of it, a kind of traveling which we know can be as fraught as it is joyful and complex. Yes, perhaps we want it to seem as if we danced all the way home. But that is an illusion that takes every resource we have, an admixture of skill and experience. My title is derived from William Meredith's love poem, "Crossing Over." His speaker is on an ice floe in the middle of a river, *in danger*. He says he loves "this fool's walk. / The thing we have to learn is how to walk light." I love that fool's walk too. Like Meredith's speaker, in spite of what I know, I "go out on it anyhow." The memoirs that are interspersed, I trust, are entrees into a mentality that may partially account for such seminal foolishness.

Stepping Out

IN HEINRICH BOLL'S, "THE BALEK SCALES," AN ARCHETYPAL STORY
that dramatizes how the powerful keep power, the Baleks, who run the
feudal town, create and perpetuate the myth that Bilgan the Giant lives
in the woods. This keeps the townspeople out of the woods, beyond
which is a town that has scales. There's only one scale in the Baleks'
town, and they own it. It's rigged. The townspeople bring in mush-
rooms and other produce from the fields, the scale determines how
much they will be paid. On one of its most significant levels, the story
is about simple heroism: A young boy, sensing dishonesty, dares to go
through the woods to find the evidence for his suspicions. Without a
clear sense of where he's going, he locates the distant town and finds
out the exact degree (in ounces) by which he's been cheated, and brings
the truth back to the people who are changed by it.

It is one of the greatest stories I know about the link between greed
and power and injustice. In addition to perpetuating the self-serving
myth of Bilgan the Giant and also controlling the town's industry, the
Baleks "own" the police, and they have the priest in the philosophical
pocket. The Baleks certainly knew how to do it—economic, military,
and clerical control, with a scary story to keep the folks at home: a
model for an empire. An all too familiar model. The story raises a cru-
cial political question: How do you behave when there is only one game
in town and you learn that game is fixed? For centuries, the variously
oppressed have answered that question in much the same way. They be-
have "badly" at first, out of anger, and they are suppressed and/or killed.
Resignation sets in for some of the survivors. But gradually and inex-
orably, others plan, gather forces, and, after many years and with great

travail, succeed or set in motion the apparatus of change. Boll, however, attempts no more than to give us the structure of a tyranny, a heroic catalyst in the boy, and the first rush of outrage by the newly informed populace. The Baleks defeat the townspeople's small, impetuous revolution, but the story ends with the truth, through word of mouth, being passed on.

Boll's elemental tale would satisfy and enlighten even if I hadn't had the childhood I had, but for me it evoked a time when I was constricted and tempted by neighborhood parameters, both real and mythical. For my purposes, it's the boy and his ability to transcend his environment — the boy as emblematic poet — toward whom this memoir will meander and finally concern itself.

Always there were parental admonitions, Don't go beyond Groton Street, Don't hang around with the troublemakers, Don't accept invitations from strangers, by which I was more or less guided. My parents were benign Baleks, but all Baleks — benign or evil — must be resisted if we are to find out who we are. As I grew older, parental admonitions blended with and finally gave way to neighborhood legends. Our Bilgan the Giant had many faces; enough kids had gotten hurt in various parts of the kingdom to prove it. When you stepped out of your neighborhood you had to know where you were, how to move, and how to get back home. The problem was, of course, that you needed experience to know such things, and our cautionary legends militated against having foreign experiences. In this sense, we were our own Baleks.

I grew up as a Catholic in the Jewish section of Forest Hills, New York, a relatively safe middle-class neighborhood, and "foreign" constituted a few blocks in any direction. Four or five blocks to the south was Metropolitan Avenue, the beginning of the Italian neighborhood. To the west, Yellowstone Boulevard marked an area of mixed ethnicity — poorer kids and their street gang, the Gauchos. To the east, beyond Continental Avenue, were the harmless Protestants, but to the north, near Our Lady Queen of Martyrs and Queens Boulevard, were a handful of tough Irish Catholics and notably a boy named Crocker, Bilgan the Giant incarnate. (It was rumored that Crocker had killed someone in a knife fight.) Back then Crocker was called a juvenile delinquent; today, he'd be a sociopath. Blacks lived two subway stops away in

Jamaica, Queens – it might as well have been Idaho. My Jewish friends and I knew at least one telling story about each group, enough to keep us near home. Mostly.

But close to home there were worries, too. Every neighborhood has bullies, and I'm convinced that they watch how we walk. In Forest Hills, shufflers were in deep trouble, as were the pigeon-toed. Kids who walked like ducks were doomed. (Girls always were in some danger no matter how they walked, but that's another subject, too large and complicated to discuss here.) Kids who bounced when they walked were in less trouble, but rarely were taken seriously. A loose-limbed, jaunty, I'm-cool kind of walk almost always signaled someone who talked too much. He'd get in trouble with his mouth. And a straight, ramrod-up-the-ass walk suggested either terror of simply being alive, or some desperate need to be in control, which probably amount to the same thing. Bullies would flick lighted matches at those kids, would try to make them dance on command.

Walking wrong: I had some sense of it even as a kid. I tried to cultivate a walk that would give away none of the above. I think my walk was somewhere in between "Walking tall," like the best movie heroes, and walking quietly, like a medium-sized animal, a vegetarian, trying not to disturb his natural enemy. Above all, I tried not to let my false confidence ring false.

When I was in seventh grade I often had to walk past Jackie Sternberg, a sinewy, cruel older boy who like to punch kids in the arm. He tried to hit me in the biceps, which in most of us had not yet developed. I think he liked to see the resulting bruise, as if it were something he could measure himself by. "Want a knuckle sandwich?" he'd say, and wouldn't wait for an answer. I was careful not to hesitate as I walked past his favorite spot in the school yard, and was careful to look at him directly, but not too directly. Jackie understood the averted eye as well as he did a limp. He also understood that if you said, "Hi, Jackie," it was a sign of fear. He was a classic bully, I think a lawyer now. He never hit me. I don't know what I would have done if he had.

Perhaps the fact that I didn't get hit had more to do with how tall I was for my age than it did with brilliant walking. I was five-ten by the time I was twelve, skinny, but well-coordinated. I suppose this was why

I became president of the Cobras. We were a team, actually, not a gang. Therefore, getting those blue-and-gold satin jackets with "Cobras" on the back was a mistake. Within two weeks, Marty, our second baseman, was chased by a few of the Italians. Ronnie was beaten up by the Gauchos, his arm broken. He had walked one street too far, looking wrong, probably even walking wrong. We sent the jackets back to the store, had "Athletic Club" sewn below "Cobras." None of us was mistaken for a rival gang member again.

In the case of the Cobras and our unwise jackets, I'm speaking as much about the value of tact (a minor aspect of style) as I am about survival strategies or their absence. Tact implies an awareness of your audience. We had all been too self-involved to know what a name like Cobras would mean to the Gauchos. Ours was a failure to understand the resonance of language and its social significance. Yet the underside of tact is that those who master it can become too careful, can give up important aspects of self just to temporize, get along. Had we sacrificed identity by sending the jackets back? In fact, we told ourselves, we really were an athletic club. We were modifying our language in the direction of the truth.

Those of us who write know that the modest claim is usually more credible (and therefore safer) than the grand one. But we must admit that its attendant pleasures are necessarily that much smaller. There's the trade-off. The grand claim, stylistically and substantively earned, is a rare phenomenon, therefore a worthy one. Our stature, however, required tact. By contrast, the Gauchos *were* the Gauchos. They had a fist behind every jacket. They walked boldly, and in numbers. One can say that they had a style equal to their intentions.

Yet, as we know, such matters are relative. A year after Ronnie's broken arm, the Gauchos lost a rumble to the Panthers from nearby Corona. I don't know if the Panthers had style, but they did have substance: more members, more weapons. The Gauchos were the real thing, though provincially defined. Local heroes often discover they're bums when they move to the next-higher league. Worse is when they don't know there *is* a next league, and a league above it. The Gauchos lacked, finally, a sense of dimension. Blake was on the mark when he said that you have to know what's more than enough in order to know what's enough.

The style Richie Goldstein and I affected when we tried to nonchalant our way past Crocker and his boys served none of our intentions. We were walking home from the movies. Ahead of us, in front of the White Castle, was a bunch of rowdies, openly drinking beer. That much we could see. It was one of those they've-seen-us, lets-not-show-them-we're-afraid situations. Richie and I decided to brazen it out (with our best out-for-a-stroll gait). But when we got closer we saw Bilgan and his boys. Crocker wore his blond hair Elvis-style. And he had a package of cigarettes rolled up in the shoulder of his T-shirt in the tough-guy style of the period. This accentuated his muscles. It was too late to turn around, even though I said in a half-whisper, "That's Crocker," and Richie mumbled something like, "Oh, no."

They got silent as we approached, backed off to let us pass. We were about twenty feet beyond then when Cocker yelled, "Let's get the kikes," and seconds later I felt a boot strike me in the back of my upper thigh. Richie was on the track team; he got away. I ran, too, but they caught me after a block and dragged me into a doorway. They kicked me a few times and I remember Crocker saying, "Take this, you dirty Jew." But one of his boys said, "Wait, I know this guy from school, his name is Dunn. He ain't a Jew." Crocker stopped kicking me to ask if that was true. It was three-quarters true (my maternal grandfather was Jewish), and I said "I'm not Jewish." There are ways to rationalize such a desperate response, but I still wince a little when I think that I allowed Crocker and his gang to think I was more like them than Richie. Crocker helped me up, asked if I wanted a beer. It was his form of apology.

I headed toward home, relieved and ashamed, and rang Richie Goldstein's doorbell. His mother answered, ashen-faced. Richie was hiding behind the sofa, but came out when he heard it was me. All his life his family had told him stories of the Nazis. He had finally met one, and so had I. When I saw his face, I lied to him, told him that I, too, had gotten cleanly away. At that moment, did I understand what collaboration meant? Did I understand how appallingly simple it can be? I can't remember.

Guilt aside, nonchalance is a bad tactic with certain theorists. If the theory says Jews must be killed, or some equal aberration, evasive action might make sense. Acting nonchalant is stupid. The more we know about history, the more we know that in such circumstances we must forget about subtlety, forget even about poetry if we are poets, and attack the theory and its proponents. I've always admired George Oppen, who, because he felt he couldn't do both, gave up writing poetry in the 1930s in order to be a political activist. I take this as evidence that he had too much respect for poetry to be polemical with it. And too much commitment to changing the conditions of the world to permit himself the ambiguities that poets must honor. Such ambiguities would have prevented him from being single-minded, and he must have needed to be single-minded just then. When Oppen returned to writing poems twenty-five years later, there was no nonsense and much substance behind his lean and jagged style.

Oppen, I think, would have known that your most subtle moves don't work very well when you don't know where you are. Richie and I had been in Crocker territory, and we acted as if we were dealing with Jackie Sternberg in a Jewish school yard. A political error.

To know where you are requires imagination. To move well requires skill. Behind both, optimally, should be a sense of history. Concomitantly, you need nerve and/or a keen Darwinian fear. The boy in "The Balek Scales" had everything but a sense of history. He didn't know that the weak, without weapons and careful planning, always lose to the strong. On the other hand, he can be likened to the great religious figures and the brave thinkers. He went ahead anyway, in the face of enormous odds. The difference between a politician and a radical is that the politician seeks consensus. The radical usually is too driven and impatient to wait for the committee's vote. Radicals originate. Politicians implement. The boy was an emblem for knowing where one is (under the collective thumb of the Baleks), and seeing through what passes for the truth. Also he's an emblem for the virtues of risking getting lost. Bilgan the Giant didn't exist, a fact he couldn't know, and it took supreme courage to venture far enough to confirm that.

The great poets, it seems to me, have slain more giants that never existed than ones that did. On one level, this means that we live with

various mystifications — like religious dogma or government-speak —
against which almost any honest poem is a corrective. On another level,
more parallel to the boy's quest, the non-existent giants fall as poets suc-
cessfully reconcile their ways of seeing and feeling with external reali-
ties. Such reconciliations cast a light. They clarify and disabuse.

My early New York peregrinations have driven me to want to know
at all times where I am. As this pertains to my writing, I'm capable, at
best, of a keen and useful alertness to the landscapes of my poems. But
needing to have such surety is something I must work against. Some-
times it's desirable, indeed necessary, to move without a compass. A
poem can die if there's no departure from the known place. Therefore,
I've learned that I need, now and then, to get myself in a little trouble.
Insert a foreign detail. Say something I can't yet support, or even fully
understand. In a sense, to step out of my neighborhood. If I'm not lost
after I've gotten lost, I may have something to talk about and a new place
from which to say it.

Recently I was in Atlantic City, and made the kind of walking error
that suggests I'm not as careful or street-wise as I'd like to think. It was
late, raining. I was returning from Resorts International, the casino I
often frequent. My car was parked two blocks away. The quickest way
to it was through an alley. Why, knowing the neighborhood as I did,
would I choose the quickest, not the safest, way? (My choice was proof
that I didn't quite know where I was, or didn't sufficiently care.) I had
my rubber raincoat on, the hood up. A black man walked toward me
from the other side of the alley. He was middle-aged, tall, bareheaded in
the rain. I saw him. He saw me. We gave each other room, each of us
wary, walking like crabs: slow, sideways while going forward. As we
neared each other, he said, "Don't mess with me. I have a gun at home."
I held up my hands, as if to communicate "No problem." When I got to
my car, I was shaking. Later, I loved recalling that he said he had a gun
at home. That was style, of a sort, in search of substance, and I loved
thinking that you're in trouble if you leave your substance home. There's
nothing to be proud of in this instance. But if I hadn't walked foolishly,
I'd have one less story to tell and embellish.

The adult situation that arose most inevitably out of my childhood
occurred in Syracuse several years ago. It was the White Castle and

Crocker revisited, and it may go to prove that Santayana's truism has a flip side: Sometimes one who fully understands his history is doomed to repeat it.

Galenti, my neighbor, the biker, the drug dealer, was sitting on the stoop with a pistol in his hand. I was about fifty yards from the house when I saw him. Somehow I knew he was waiting for me. My first impulse was to pivot, go in another direction. But, like Crocker that night, he had seen me. Once again I reasoned that the best course of action was to show that I wasn't afraid. I used my walking tall, medium-sized, animal walk.

This was Syracuse, and I was a thirty-year-old graduate student at the university. I lived in a poor part of town in an old house with thin walls. The gun-toter lived in the other apartment on the ground floor, and we shared a common basement. In the winter, he kept his motorcycle down there. A few months earlier he had almost strangled the upstairs neighbor for blocking the driveway. A month after that I had called the Humane Society because he was repeatedly mistreating his dog. They had taken her away. Did he know that I had placed the call?

"I was waiting for you," he said as I approached. "There's a goddamn sparrow in the basement. Been shitting on my bike. I want to shoot it, but the bullets might go up into your living room. Is that a problem?" It was a relief that *I* wasn't the problem, and, though still afraid, I said no, but I would catch the sparrow for him. That I did, trapped it with a pillow up against the rafters, transferred it to my hand, and took it out into the sunlight, where it burst open my hand and gloriously flew away.

I could have been shot. But if I had backed away after he had seen me, I think he would have made my life miserable from then on. Did I know where I was? Maybe yes, maybe no. It could be said that I knew existential territory better than I did the political territory. After all, I was walking into a situation where I had no power and few resources. If he'd been inclined to harm me, I had made it easy for him. On the other hand, he could harm me anytime he wanted. Something about living on my own terms impelled me forward. Was it a good decision? Well, it worked. But empiricism is a lousy way to determine the value of an act. The boy in "The Balek Scales" failed empirically, succeeded as a beacon, a spirit. The Baleks were exposed as scum, the fixers and cheaters of the world. I saved a sparrow because I was afraid to show I was afraid.

Inherent in "The Balek Scales" is that one must walk wrong in order to walk right. The boy did everything wrong—according to the prevailing ethos of his society. Crocker also did everything wrong. But Crocker sought nothing beyond the viscera of his malice. Knowledge would have cramped his style. The boy walked wrong in pursuit of knowledge and toward an eventual justice he could only intuit. His style —as emblematic poet—if he can be said to have a style, is inseparable from his convictions and his deeds. It could be called clean, efficient, a style which properly drew little attention to itself. As a poet he'd have been a Hardy rather than, say, a Keats.

The story as a whole sticks with me, prods me. I think it says to me that you have to know where you are, but that that's just the beginning of useful consciousness. Then you have to go where you can't.

In life, as in art, there are many ways to get where you can't, very few of them heroic. On such journeys it is not unusual to find tact and chicanery, not to mention innocence, complicating courage and moral intelligence. But good stories make us dream. The boy in "The Balek Scales" is who we might be whenever we hear some inner voice and trust it, and go with it as far as we can imagine.

※

Bringing the Strange Home

Czeslaw Milosz, in his book of essays *The Witness of Poetry*, eloquently states one of the dilemmas facing the modern poet:

> When poets discover that their words refer only to other words and not to reality which must be described as faithfully as possible, they despair. This is probably one cause for modern poetry's somber tone. In addition, poets are threatened by isolation. The bond between them and "the great human family" was still intact in the era of romanticism, that is, the Renaissance pattern of fame, gratitude from, and recognition by others was still operative. Later, when poetry moved underground and bohemia turned away with scorn from the philistines, it found serious support in the idea of Art with a capital A, its absolute meaningfulness. Poetry entered the twentieth century convinced of a fundamental antagonism between Art and the world, but Art's fortress was already crumbling and the sense of the poet's superiority to ordinary mortals had began to lose its highest justification.

Later in his book, Milosz defines poetry as "the passionate pursuit of the real." So, we have a problem. The poet, in most countries, is divorced in large or small degree from the great human family. And if we concur with Milosz's definition, that "poetry is the passionate pursuit of the real," to whom then is the poet speaking about the reality he or she seeks? To other poets? To everyone who is not a philistine? And does it matter to whom the poet is speaking?

In the twentieth century we are confronted by a reality that is often, again in Milosz's words, "too atrocious to think of." And we are equally confronted by a reality of ordinariness composed of boredom and routine, domestic quarrels, pleasures, etc. Both realities and all the other realities in between, are important. The problem is not so much that people in our culture inure themselves to the horrors of the world, which is understandable; it's that they don't believe poetry speaks to the conditions of their lives and thus have inured themselves to the possibility that it can.

Poetry, as we know, is not very important to people in the United States. In addition to Milosz's observations, the reasons for this are complex and reside deeply in the culture; among them are the capitalist privileging of acquisition over contemplation, the celebration of things more than matters of the soul, a general awkwardness that culminates in value being defined in monetary terms. And, to be fair, the amount of poetry that *doesn't* have much to do with our lives.

There are, of course, the great poems of the tradition to turn to. But even for the intelligent, willing reader, those poems too often smack of tortuous lessons in school, and the breaking of some secret code. Besides, the great poems are poems we need to get ready for by reading many poems, good, great, and otherwise. The important thing is to find poems that truly matter to us. There are many strong contemporary poets to turn to, but if would-be readers make the wrong turn, once again they'll think poetry has little to do with their lives. Even those of us who pay close attention to poetry are regularly confronted with poems we can't understand, poems with unlocatable voices, unlocatable concerns. On the other hand, we are equally besieged by poems that are so clear we wish they weren't, that seem to insist that the poet's personal experiences are *ipso facto* interesting and significant.

So there's a gulf, not just between the poet and the philistine (not much we can do about that), but between the poet and the willing, intelligent reader as well. And there are the countless others out there who fall somewhere in the unconscious middle, hungry for meaning in their lives, in need of poetry, yet unaware of it. It is with them and the willing, intelligent (non-poet) readers that this essay concerns itself, but it is primarily addressed to those of you, poets and those dedicated to poetry, who might worry about the antagonism between art and the populace.

What should poetry offer us? What should it do? There are many possible answers to these questions, but let me suggest a very general proposition which is surely not new. Poetry should offer us something we can believe about ourselves and the world, or it should offer us something that will provoke or suggest contemplation about ourselves and the world.

As we know, experience is ambiguous, inchoate. Reality is some amalgam of the seer and the seen or, as the case may be, the unseen. To believe in the efficacy of poetry we have to be a little lonely for those words, images, and stories, those precisions, which speak to the inherent ambiguities and mysteries of our lives. Then, as rereaders, we have to be pleased, almost anew, by all the poem's felicities and by the issues it explores, evokes, but of course doesn't solve. If we "believe" a poem, it is because the voice behind it and the rhythms in it have become inseparable from its assertions and claims. Thus, to reread a poem that we already believe is to give ourselves a chance to refine and/or question what we believe.

It's amazing when someone gets the world right. It's a triumph of seeing and feeling and thinking and, finally, of art—the orchestrating and shaping of experience. For as much as there might be a loneliness for the conditions of our lives to be provocatively addressed, it isn't enough (for the serious reader) to address those conditions without giving us the pleasures of art. The beginning reader and the willing, intelligent reader are often satisfied with poem as content. That's all right. So are we, really. It's just that we're more difficult to please, have been tasting the wine for years, and have a more discriminating sense of what content involves, not the least of which is the arrangement of detail. For all of us, though, poems must be clear, by which I mean they must repay our attention to them. They shouldn't cover territory that's already clear. That's banality and platitude. They must make available the strangeness that is our lives. By this I mean not much more than how most of us find ourselves at odds with official versions of things, with images that, say, come from TV, from advertisements, from the daily language used to describe us. We can go months, even years, without ever being crucially spoken to. The simplest good poem is a small correction of that, and may seem difficult or strange because of what regularly passes for the truth.

For most of us, however, the strange, the aberrant, is so fully a part of what we consider the real that our poems can speak as if that strangeness were a given. The surreal exists on the front page of every newspaper, even conservative ones. Poems, I think, have to be true to the fact. But they need to defamiliarize what we already know while they are talking about the familiar. This is the burden of readers, to make their "home" hospitable for such visits.

William Carlos Williams said, "It's difficult to get the news from poems, but men die miserably every day for lack of what is found there." Yes. And here's the rub for the average reader: It's difficult sometimes to get the news from poetry because poetry is not just information. It's an arrangement, a rearrangement if you will, of experience and the world; it speaks often in metaphor, it has devices and schemes, which suggest that a poem's "news" is always more than its extractable meaning. What we must remember is that the poet is always mediating experience, and through tone, diction, texture, etc., is conferring value (or absence of it), and therefore the meaning of any poem is a combination of those things that have worked on us. It's never quite as simple, of course, as "Happiness is…" or "Prufrock means…"

Well, you know all that. Here are some poems that lately I've been reading out loud to others. The listen-to-this-isn't-it-wonderful impulse that has its roots in poetry's reason for being: the creation and explanation of the mysteries of the tribe through memorable speech, song, and story. That is, I want to speak to you as if we are all part of the same human family.

The first is by Goethe, translated by Robert Bly.

THE HOLY LONGING

> Tell a wise person, or else keep silent,
> because the massman will mock it right away.
> I praise what is truly alive,
> What longs to be burned to death.
>
> In the calm water of the love-nights,
> where you were begotten, where you have begotten,
> a strange feeling comes over you
> when you see the silent candle burning.
>
> Now you are no longer caught
> in the obsession with darkness,

and a desire for higher love-making
sweeps you upward.

Distance does not make you falter,
now, arriving in magic, flying,
and, finally, insane for the light,
you are the butterfly and you are gone.

And so long as you haven't experienced
this: to die and so to grow,
you are only a troubled guest
on the dark earth.

On one level this is a poem about good sex, and it tries to illustrate with sexual terms what it means to exceed yourself, or to obliterate self so that there might be growth of some kind.

The poem, of course, has its readily extractable meanings. You must die in order to grow. And if you don't, you are just a troubled guest on the dark earth. But through its rhythms and tone it suggests that the process can be magical as well as frightening, and that this is linked to some essential mystery. Most readers will accede to the "strange feeling" that comes over them now and then during lovemaking, or even while sitting in the living room. In this case, it is the desire for "higher love-making," a positive thing, that sweeps the person upward where the danger is. Goethe's compression of detail, his art of linking ordinary experience with the magical, is at the heart of this poem's power. But the poem begins, "Tell a wise person, or else keep silent / because the massman will mock it right away." To the extent that we are "massmen" the poem is a criticism of us and a challenge, though one of Goethe's tricks is to link us with the author and the wise. But if we're honest we know how many times we've put aside or stopped thinking about our "strange feelings" and gone on with our lives in the great middle, never all the way up or all the way down.

I praise what is truly alive,
what longs to be burned to death.

Well, yes, as long as we don't lose our jobs and still have a flight home. The massman (philistine) might mock this poem, not because he doesn't understand it, but because if he were to read it he might sense it's a criticism of him. But there's no doubt the poem is speaking to his life. The poem is the more terrifying the more one subscribes uncritically to middleclass values (e.g., comfort, safety at all costs). The more we subscribe to them the greater the danger of being separated from our souls, if you'll excuse such a big word. The more, in other words, we become separated from ourselves. Paul Valéry wrote, "I believe in all sincerity that if each man were not able to live a number of lives beside his own, he would not be able to live his own life." The point then can be extended: not just the danger of being separated from ourselves, but the danger of being separated from otherness.

I like the word "only" in the last sentence: "…you are only a troubled guest / on the dark earth." The "only" suggests that to be a troubled guest is a normal condition, and that you might have many other identities at the same time. But to be only a troubled guest is of course a particularly sad identity. Notice that Goethe doesn't resort to any easy or melodramatic causalities, such as "you will become a troubled guest," as a lesser poet might have. The choice of "only" arises out of a considered philosophical disposition, and allows us to trust the author while somewhat mitigating the didactic nature of the poem. The poem, of course, doesn't suggest any methods, is not a how-to tract for improvement. It is offered without program, and supported by language which serves to defamiliarize us from similar and pedestrian notions on the subject. It is intimately about our lives and our inarticulate longings. It requires, to read it right (I'd argue), more bravery than intelligence, though you might have to know how far to take a metaphor, as Frost says we must, to read it just right. I prefer poems, as you'll see, which, instead of thumbing their noses at the bourgeoisie, confront it and us, return us to the strange, which, when delivered, takes its place next to the peanut butter and jelly on the table.

Another poem that lately I've felt impelled to read to people is less confrontational than "The Holy Longing" and not strange in the conventional use of the word: "Next Day" by Randall Jarrell. Its female speaker is as middle-class as you can get, and the words Jarrell gives her are apparently simple and straightforward, though perhaps deceptively so.

NEXT DAY

Moving from Cheer to Joy, from Joy to All,
I take a box
And add it to my wild rice, my Cornish game hens.
The slacked or shorted, basketed, identical
Food-gathering flocks
Are selves I overlook. Wisdom, said William James,

Is learning what to overlook. And I am wise
If that is wisdom.
Yet somehow, as I buy All from these shelves
And the boy takes it to my station wagon,
What I've become
Troubles me even if I shut my eyes.

When I was young and miserable and pretty
And poor, I'd wish
What all girls wish: to have a husband,
A house and children. Now that I'm old, my wish
is womanish:
That the boy putting groceries in my car

See me. It bewilders me he doesn't see me.
For so many years
I was good enough to eat; the world looked at me
And its mouth watered. How often they have undressed me,
The eyes of strangers!
And, holding their flesh within my flesh, their vile

Imaginings within my imagining,
I too have taken
The chance of life. Now the boy pats my dog
And we start home. Now I am good.
The last mistaken,
Ecstatic, accidental bliss, the blind

Happiness that, bursting, leaves upon the palm
Some soap and water —
It was so long ago, back in some Gay
Twenties, Nineties, I don't know…Today I miss

My lovely daughter
Away at school, my sons away at school,

My husband away at work — I wish for them.
The dog, the maid,
And I go through the sure unvarying days
At home in them. As I look at my life,
I am afraid
Only that it will change, as I am changing:

I am afraid, this morning, of my face.
It looks at me
From the rear-view mirror, with the eyes I hate,
The smile I hate. Its plain, lined look
Of gray discovery
Repeats to me: "You're old." That's all, I'm old.

And yet I'm afraid, as I was at the funeral
I went to yesterday.
My friend's cold made-up face, granite among its flowers,
Her undressed, operated-on, dressed body
Were my face and body.
As I think of her I hear her telling me

How young I seem; I am exceptional;
I think of all I have.
But really no one is exceptional,
No one has anything, I'm anybody,
I stand beside my grave
Confused with my life, that is commonplace and solitary.

It seems to me that if we went around the country reading this poem at churches, at various social gatherings, we would persuade a few more people that poetry has something to do with their lives. The genius of the poem is how effortlessly it conceals its artfulness, its elaborate patterning, its adroit rhymes. The poem is not written in natural speech. Few successful poems are. But it does give the illusion of natural speech.

Wallace Stevens wrote that "the poem must be the cry of its occasion," and for a long time we don't know what this poem's occasion is. We don't know why the woman is moved to so evaluate her life until, late in the poem, we learn that she went to her friend's funeral the day before. At this point we recognize the brilliance of the title. Though this poem is not strange in any way, Jarrell has nevertheless acknowledged something fundamental and hidden about this woman's life. She's bewildered, confused, and full of small recognitions that seemingly astound her. She has begun, one might argue, to live the examined life, has become reconnected to her soul, though of course these deepenings are not altogether sanguine. She, in a different way of looking at her, is the paradigm of the middle-class person ready for poetry: alert, attuned, needy, perhaps even ready to die in order to grow. Jarrell permits us to overhear her, and it's difficult not to be moved.

The extractable meanings are less available in this poem because we feel we've overheard—from the inside out—a person in crisis, as opposed to ideas about a person in crisis. She tells her story and we listen. The more sophisticated of us are aware, however, of the inherent extra pleasures of poetry—language and music—beyond the poem's information. Probably everyone who reads or hears the poem is aware, on some level, of the pleasures in

> The slacked or short, basketed, identical
> Food-gathering flocks...

in among the flat, less-stressed, normative language of the poem. And we are pleased when, at just the right interval, Jarrell allows her to say

> The last mistaken,
> Ecstatic, accidental bliss, the blind
> Happiness that, bursting, leaves upon the palm...

And once again, some twenty lines later,

> My friend's cold made-up face, granite among its flowers,
> Her undressed, operated-on, dressed body
> Were my face and body.

These are the pleasures of textural and rhythmical promises fulfilled surprisingly, and of the poem's architecture. When we read it closely, we see the entire pattern of recurrences on which the poem is based, and perhaps understand why we felt so easily drawn into it. Not just the rhythm and architecture of the poem, but tacitly the poem offering the rhythm and architecture of a life.

The painter Edward Hopper said he was pleased with his work "when the facts are given unity by my interests and prejudices." Hopper's painting would be mere realism without those prejudices and interests. But "unity" may even be the more important word. Without his quest for unity, his paintings might be like the kinds of poems in which information is thought to be sufficient. The audience for art need not be compositionally sophisticated, but the artist must be, even if that sophistication is intuitive rather than raised to principle. Hopper's paintings, the houses, the landscapes, the people in stark rooms (all apparently simple) have a strangeness because they are so infused with Hopper's attitudes toward them that we're mostly aware that we're looking at a Hopper; reality mediated by one person's powerful sensibility and art.

The poems I'm drawn to are equally (un)simple, and are infused with the same imposition of sensibility on material. I think of "Next Day" as a Jarrell, as one might speak of a Hopper, though Hopper's signature is stronger. I've been given not a middle-aged woman, but a version of a middle-aged woman, and, beyond that and mostly, the curve and curves of a particular sensibility, Jarrell's. It is important for us who care about poetry to know that this poem is an illusion, artifice. It is also important for us to be utterly seduced by its literal surface on first reading.

William Carpenter's poem "Rain" signals from its outset that it's going to balance strange and commonplace details and rather openly announces itself as a fiction. Carpenter's a poet who's assimilated the surrealists' techniques and angles of vision, and is able to use them without strain in service of quotidian experience.

RAIN

A man stood in the rain outside his house.
Pretty soon, the rain soaked through
his jacket and shirt. He might have
gone in, but he wanted to be wet, to be
really wet, so that it finally got through
his skin and began raining on the rooftops
of the small city that the man always carried
inside him, a city where it hadn't rained

for thirty years, only now the sky darkened
and tremendous drops fell in the thick dust
of the streets. The man's wife knocked
on the window, trying to call him in.
She twirled one finger around her ear
to sign that he was crazy, that he'd
get sick again, standing in street clothes
in a downpour. She put the finger in her mouth
like a thermometer. She formed the word *idiot*
with her lips, and, always, when she said that
he would give in. But now he stood there.
His whole life he'd wanted to give something,
to sacrifice. At times he'd felt like coming up
to people on the street, offering his blood.
Here, you look like you need blood. Take mine.
Now he could feel the people of his city
waking as if from a long drought. He could feel
them leaving their houses and jobs, standing
with their heads up and their mouths open,
and the little kids taking their clothes off
and lying on their bellies in the streams
and puddles formed by the new rain that the man
made himself, not by doing anything, but standing
there while the rain soaked through his clothes.
He could see his wife and his own kids
staring from the window, the younger kid
laughing at his crazy father, the older one
sad, almost in tears, and the dog, Ossian—
but the man wanted to drown in the city in rain.
He wanted the small crowded apartments
and the sleazy taverns to empty their people
into the streets. He wanted a single man with
an umbrella to break out dancing the same way
Gene Kelly danced in Singing in the Rain,
then another man, and more, until the whole
city was doing turns and pirouettes with their
canes or umbrellas, first alone, then taking
each other by the arm and waist, forming a larger
and larger circle in the square, and not
to any music but to the percussion of the rain
on the roof of his own house. And if there were
a woman among the dancers, a woman in a flowery

>   print skirt, a woman wetter and happier and more
>   beautiful than the rest, may this man be
>   forgiven for falling in love on a spring
>   morning in the democracy of the rain, may
>   he be forgiven for letting his family think
>   that is just what to expect from someone who
>   is every day older and more eccentric, may he
>   be forgiven for evading his responsibilities, for growing
>   simple in the middle of his life, for
>   ruining his best pants and his one decent tie.

A man standing in the rain outside of his house has a city inside him where it hasn't rained in thirty years, and the rain is raining into him and his city, as he desires it to, while his family watches unsympathetically. There, that should prove forever how inadequate it is to paraphrase a poem. The poem's success resides with how adroitly Carpenter combines the fantastical with the commonplace, and how he's able to signal his readers from the beginning that they're in good hands, by which I mean that the lines

>   He might have
>   gone in, but he wanted to be wet, to be
>   really wet, so that it finally got through
>   his skin...

introduce them (us) to desires that suggest a theme, and promise more than fanciful invention. The scene of the man standing in the rain is conventional enough, maybe just mildly aberrant, but the man's desires and feelings about his arid inner life inform us that the poem will work itself out psychologically. If we can accept that, and I'm sure most of us can, then the poem is not particularly strange at all. Carpenter simply has to extend the poem's imaginative logic. But there are two levels on which the poem progresses. One, with the exaggerations that are psychological evidence of the man's neediness. The other, the wife and the family's very realistic reactions to the man's actions. We may say that the strange is constantly being normalized because of this interplay. Tonally, Carpenter is conferring degrees of value on what he's describing. Overall, the tone is comic, masking but not obscuring the poem's serious intent. This tone is appropriate because Carpenter knows one man's mid-life crisis is another person's situation comedy, and that the lengths we will go to demonstrate our needs and sadnesses are often absurd. Yet the constant charm of the details make us sympathetic to a man trying not to be a troubled guest in his own world.

"Rain," the word, the phenomenon, from the beginning, has been evocative of vitality, and the word keeps on accruing in meaning. Dancing in the rain is a credible evolution of such vitality, and the scene enlarges to include many dancers, one of whom is "wetter and happier and more / beautiful than the rest" and represents the dream-wish of a man alienated from his domestic environment, the wetness now clearly sexual, if lightly so. The woman is eroticized by her own movements and the eyes of admirers; she's a woman fully alive (as opposed to the wife who out of propriety has chided him). It is all so obviously vibrant to the man that the narrator wishes that the man be forgiven for falling in love in "the democracy of rain," where, as in the imagination, all things are possible. The poem, in its extractable meaning, is a dramatization of a man trying to save himself, but in its particularities has managed to delight us with its story and management of detail. To reduce the poem to its "meaning" is to lose that delightfulness.

In general terms, "Rain" presents to us the somewhat desperate and comic imagination (of the poet) and of a man in minor crisis. It is a fiction, by which I mean something for us to believe, something that is an analogue to experience, a system of language with an interior logic. All of its strangeness is normalized, brought home.

Ellen Bryant Voigt also has written a poem in which dancing is used as a figure for eliminating distance and alienation.

DANCING WITH POETS

"The accident" is what he calls the time
he threw himself from a window four floors up,
breaking his back and both ankles, so that walking
became the direst labor for this man
who takes my hand, invites me to the empty strip of floor
that fronts the instruments, a length of polished wood
the shape of a grave. Unsuited for this world —
his body bears the marks of it, his hand

is tense with effort and with shame, and I shy away
from any audience, but I love to dance, and soon
we find a way to move, drifting apart as each
effects a different ripple across the floor,
a plaid and a stripe to match the solid navy of the band.
And suddenly the band is getting better, so pleased
to have this pair of dancers, since we make evident
the music in the noise — and the dull pulse
leaps with unexpected riffs and turns, we can hear
how good the keyboard really is, the bright cresting
of another major key as others join us: a strict
block of a man, a formidable cliff of mind, dancing
as if melted, as if unhinged; his partner a gift of brave
elegance to those who watch her dance; and at her elbow,
Berryman back from the bridge, and Frost, relieved
of grievances, Dickinson waltzing there with lavish Keats,
who coughs into a borrowed handkerchief — all the poets of
exile and despair, unfit for this life, all those who cannot speak
but only sing, all those who cannot walk
who strut and spin until the waiting citizens at the bar,
aloof, judgmental, begin to sway or drum their straws
or hum, leave their seats to crowd the narrow floor
and now we are one body, sweating and foolish,
one body with its clear pathetic grace, not
lifted out of grief but dancing it, transforming
for one night this local bar, before we're turned back out
to our separate selves, to the dangerous streets and houses,
to the overwhelming drone of the living world.

In the beginning we are instantly aware of the narrator's distance from and yet empathy with the damaged person she's describing. He is someone "unsuited for this world." As the poem progresses, and this is Voigt's strategy, the distance decreases, and through the act of dancing, the implicitly "normal" narrator and the man unsuited for this world merge, publicly and joyously, until in her imagination " all the poets of exile and despair, unfit for this life," start to dance with them.

The poem, except for the summoning of the dead poets, stays with its literal, tangible, believable situation. The literal pleasures are considerable, and the poem works as a wonderful story, supported by clauses that rock back and forth against each other; motion and sound continually in cooperation with what's being described. But it's clear, too, that it is infused with intent that resonates beyond the literal.

On a second level, the poem is about poetry and its audience, the dance of poetry, and how, when right, it brings into the common fold

> ...all those who cannot speak
> but only sing, all those who cannot walk
> who strut and spin until the waiting citizens at the bar,
> aloof, judgmental, begin to sway or drum their straws
> or hum, leave their seats and crowd the narrow floor
> and now we are one body...

A lesser poet, I think, would have stopped there with this glorious moment. But Voigt knows the dance is temporary, and that the transformation is for one night

> ...before we're turned back out
> from our separate selves, to the dangerous streets and houses,
> to the overwhelming drone of the living world.

She also knows *because* we mostly live in "our separate selves" how very important the dance is, temporary or not. Berryman and Frost, Keats and Dickinson, are of course real poets, but the point is that even the "aloof, judgmental" people at the bar are part of the entire symbiotic act. The title "Dancing with Poets" collects and embraces everyone there, from the literal cripple to all those who are crippled by separateness and the drone of the danger of the world. By extension it collects and embraces all of us.

Poetry may make nothing happen, and I don't think it's desirable for it to be written as if it could make something happen. I'm just interested in those poems that manage to cut through passable truths or to another level of truth and connection. The massman may never come around to liking or understanding Voigt or these other poets, but it's not because these poems have turned away from him. We need to find and champion the poems that are true to the ambiguity of experience, the ones that will repay our attention without always sending us deep into the classroom or the code book for answers. But we also need to give ourselves over as wholly as possible to all kinds of poems, to regularly prepare ourselves for those others which legitimately ask more of us.

Here's a poem by Carlos Drummond de Andrade, translated by
Mark Strand, which as you'll see is a series of strongly asserted direct
statements, but in sum and is an arrangement, an orchestration, of a par-
ticular crossroads in a person's life.

YOUR SHOULDERS HOLD UP THE WORLD

A time comes when you no longer can say: my God.
A time of total cleaning up.
A time when you no longer can say: my love,
Because love proved useless.
And the eyes don't cry,
And the hands do only rough work.
And the heart is dry.

Women knock at your door in vain, you won't open.
You remain alone, the light turned off,
and your enormous eyes shine in the dark.
It is obvious you no longer know how to suffer.
And you want nothing from your friends.

Who cares if old age comes, what is old age?
Your shoulders are holding up the world
and it's lighter than a child's hand.
Wars, famine, family fights inside buildings
prove only that life goes on
and nobody will ever be free.

Some (the delicate ones) judging the spectacle cruel
will prefer to die.
A time comes when death doesn't help.
A time comes when life is an order.
Just life, with no escapes.

On first reading, this may be thought of as a counterstatement to
"The Holy Longing," the Goethe poem. But both poems are very much
about the same thing, staying alive. Andrade may even be articulating
for us that nadir, that death, which one must arrive at in order to grow.
Goethe's poem is, in its paradoxes, a strong antidote to suicide. "Your
Shoulders Hold Up the World" is, too, though it's less romantic, less

suggestive of growth through suffering.

> A time comes when life is an order.
> Just life, with no escapes.

Its first stanza depicts an extreme case of emotional aridity and with-drawal. The message is that it's simply important to endure, that this is the ultimate courage. Sure, you may be a troubled guest. But don't be so delicate as to want to die. Yet the poem isn't all straightforward.

> Your shoulders are holding up the world
> and it's lighter than a child's hand.

What do these lines mean? I'm not sure, though the context would tell us that they have something to do with bearing burdens, something to do with the desirability of that, that we can endure if we understand the conditions of the world, if we look with a hard, not romantic eye.

In the voice we feel and hear the emotional authority to speak such a prescriptive language. Most people are amazed that a poem can speak like that and still be a poem. They're not used to mysteries being dealt with in such a way, the meaning largely on the surface. But poets *can* say what they mean, if they are wise and skillful enough. And when they resort to metaphorical or analogic language, their poems can still be as clear as Christ's parables. That they might be more difficult, demand more of us, is of course understandable and fine. But the poet must not love difficulty. That's the solipsism of the prig, the person who believes he/she has something so precious it's worth concealing.

Behind this essay is the notion that we've lost the sense of commu-nity that once allowed a poem to speak to collective fears and joys and concerns. We're a fragmented culture, we no longer have a belief system in common, and most of us are troubled guests in one way or another. Yet our "passionate pursuits of the real" need to convince our most will-ing and intelligent readers that, however fragmented we may be, we at least share *that* reality, that our problems are essentially the same. If we don't share, say a religion, we do share an essential strangeness. And if in our poems we can bring the strange home, and bring it home with precision and surprise, we are offering a correction and, in so doing, are accomplishing a useful small thing. A poem that speaks convincingly to strangeness, to otherness, brings us and others into the common fold, even if that common fold is a place that may not hold for us safety or certainty. Who's listening? Well, we must care and not care. We must not care in the sense that we are always writing to fulfill our best sense of what a poem can be, against and in light of our predecessors. But it seems to me we must care and worry if we find that, as poets, we're talking only to each other.

I am not arguing for a proletarian poetry. Poets should not homogenize their poems, nor should they simplify their diction for the sake of wider appeal. In art, excellence is all. But I do think in the back of our minds, if not in the front, we need to believe that our poetry is for others, as many others as can make themselves hospitable to it. This implies mutual gestures: the poet asking the troubled guests and the aloof to dance, the troubled guests and the aloof preparing themselves to say yes.

Only, it seems to me, by acting as if we live in a human family can a gap between the artist and society be closed. That it can be closed may be an illusion, but as Santayana said, everything is illusion, therefore choose your favorite illusion and live by it. To write as if we live in a human family has many compositional ramifications; none of them need involve lowering our sights, or compromising our sense of art.

The Good and Not So Good

THE GOOD POEM MAY BE POLITICAL, BUT IS MORE INTERESTED IN enacting or understanding the dynamics of any human situation than it is in effecting change. Nevertheless it is a desirable, subversive act to replace what passes for truth with a more accurate/deep approximation, whether the subject is a dinner party or poverty. Precision, therefore, is more radical than passion, though precision without passing might be still another definition of a not so good poem.

The poet distracted by the possibility of effecting change is looking too far ahead to be a trustworthy witness of what's in front of him/her. It has long been said that a poet must have vision. The good poet's vision is of the here and now. The world, properly seen, becomes the future.

※

The good poem is implicitly philosophical. The not so good poem, conversely, may exquisitely describe a tree or loneliness, but if the description does not suggest an attitude toward nature, or human nature, we are left with a kind of dentist office art — devoted to decoration and the status quo.

※

The good poem is elitist, if by elitist we mean pandering to no taste lower than our own. It is not elitist in the pejorative, political sense. It does not aim to exclude. It aims to find and set a standard of truth and excellence and beauty toward which anyone can aspire.

Often the not so good poem suffers from what may be called the egalitarian error; in its desire to be compassionate and fair it becomes merely correct.

⚏

Poets must be both cocky and humble. They must trust their own assertions and observations in the face of overwhelming uncertainties. They must know their job is not to offer The Truth, but to be persuasive about their version of it. The key is in the voice. In the good poem, the voice informs us that the poet embodies what the poem asserts.

In the not so good poem, there is sometimes a discrepancy between voice and that which is said. It is the sound of tin when someone is telling us about gold.

⚏

The good poem maintains a delicate balance between strangeness and familiarity. The author must make the familiar strange enough to be re-seen or re-felt by the reader. The truth is always a little strange because the conventional world has little interest in the truth and regularly accepts packaged versions of it. But a poet should never be strange for the sake of being strange; the purveyor of such poems is at heart a sensationalist, and is insufficiently interested in the human condition.

The not so good poem may err by leaning too much toward strangeness or toward familiarity, thus giving us a false sense of the real.

⚏

The good poem informs us in ways we couldn't have been informed if the poem had not existed. It has surprises throughout, and its words and rhythms convince us they are the inevitable words and rhythms for the feelings and thoughts that the poem explores.

The not so good poem is a well-made version of these feelings and thoughts, to which we accede without astonishment.

⚷

The good poem illuminates its subject so that we can see it as the poet wished and in ways the poet could not have anticipated. It follows that such illumination is twofold: the light of the mind, which the poet employs like a miner's beam, and that other light which emanates from the words on the page in conjunction with themselves, a radiance the poet caused but does not control.

⚷

The absence of wit or humor in a body of work is understandable. For some poets the conditions of their lives and the world are too dark for such leavening elements. But the absence of language-play, even in the darkest poems, is a sign of compositional torpor.

One characteristic of certain not so good poems is a kind of unredeemed earnestness, the language suffering because the poet was suffering.

⚷

The good poem alters us a little bit, or is capable of doing so. At the least, it moves us closer to what can be known and believed about the world, and our second selves (those parts of us which always know better) store such information in the vague repository which is consciousness. We may continue to behave badly after absorbing a good poem, but it might be slightly harder to forgive ourselves.

The not so good poem often allows us to make of it what we will. It doesn't confront our sense of the world or of ourselves fundamentally enough. Once again, we are given permission not to change our lives.

⚷

The good poem arises out of necessity or discovers its necessity in the act of composition. Necessity is linked to rhythm. When a poem's rhythm is off, usually it's because the poet has not yet located what is central in his/her subject. Therefore, the most fundamental act of revision is for the poet to locate the poem's informing principle, its locus of concern.

With the not so good poem revision is mostly a cosmetic issue; this word instead of that, the poet becoming willful because what was felt or thought has no fulcrum — almost anything can be substituted for anything else.

※

The good poem allows us to believe we have a soul. In the presence of a good poem we remember/discover the soul has an appetite, and that appetite is for emotional veracity and for the unsayable. The general condition of the soul, therefore, is stoic hunger, stoic loneliness.

Paul Eluard wrote, "There is another world, and it is in this one." The not so good poem isn't able to startle us into consideration of that world. The soul is never pricked into wakefulness.

※

In a not so good poem we may be aware of the author's intelligence, imagination, skill with language, etc., but we may not feel the presence of a superior intelligence, superior imagination, a superior skill with language. In the good poem we find ourselves yielding to such a presence, to that which is larger than we are.

※

The good poem simultaneously reveals and conceals. It is in this sense that it is mysterious.

The not so good poem is often mysterious only by virtue of its concealment. Or it wears exotic clothing to hide its essential plainness.

※

All poems are formal in one way or another, but the good poem demonstrates its form in a series of satisfactions. It makes both overt and subtle promises in diction, content, structure, rhythm, tone, texture, etc. The subtle promises, when fulfilled, satisfy us most, often long before we know what they are. For example, one of the formal promises a poem makes resides in what it won't do; what can be called a poem's hidden manners. Equally pleasing is the violation of a poem's manners at intervals regular enough to suggest method.

Perhaps one aspect of a not so good poem is that it neatly fulfills its overt promises, leaving us oddly dissatisfied.

⚜

The good poet "lets in" the unruly, the difficult, the unformed – in a sense, the unmanageable – and is able to make a livable environment for them. The more the imagination can accommodate, the more chaos the poet is equal to, obviously the richer the poem.

The not so good poem may try to let in the very same elements, but is overwhelmed by them. The poem, then, is too much like one's unreconstructed life; we can learn little or nothing from it.

⚜

Not only must poets turn away from tired or dead language, they must be wary of their best ideas and all the language that was available to them before the poem began. That is, all language that hasn't been found by the language in the poem. And then even that new language should be doubted and resisted. Resistance leads to discovery. No, no, no, no, and then yes. The good poem offers us a compelling, vibrant replacement for what, in our complacency, we allowed ourselves to believe we knew and felt.

The not so good poem sometimes too easily reflects or accommodates what is available prior to the poem's inception. Its author said yes too soon.

⚜

There's no reason why an abstract poem cannot be a good poem. Though no poem purely does one or the other, the poem that appeals to the mind can be as passionate or as convincing as the poem that appeals to the senses; it simply must find ways to get around the tendency of the mind to be argumentative. In the right frame, with the right focus, the right tone, bare branches can be exciting, seductive. Even ideas about bare branches.

The not so good abstract poem does not sufficiently distract the mind—with rhythm, wit, irony, form, etc.—from thinking of contraries. The mind says this poem is too spare. Why aren't there leaves?

※

For a personal poem written in the first person to be good the poet must work against the dangerous tendencies of the "I"—self-congratulation, solipsism, untransformed confession. To the extent the poet believes that the experience rendered in the poem is peculiar to him/herself, the poem will be tainted with narcissism. Details often will be chosen because they "happened," rather than because they arise out of the imperatives of the material. This is to say that the good personal poem is to some degree always fictive.

The not so good personal poem makes us feel uncomfortable the way the problems of strangers do. We're not quite sure why they're telling us what they're telling us. At best, the problem is interesting, but we feel more like voyeurs than listeners who have some stake in what we're being told.

※

There are many types of good poems, but two broad types might be worth isolating: (1) The poem in which the poet is still involved in the struggle that the poem explores, which gives us the experience of the struggle. (2) The poem in which the poet has passed through and gotten beyond his/her subject matter, the poem of maximum perspective.

In the first, the poet suggests no way out, but rather reports, registers, evaluates, thus "making" the conditions of a recognizable world so that we can better feel and see them. This is the poem we often feel most close to, as if written by a profound comrade. Generally it is more interested in what living in the world truly feels like than in what it means, though the former goes a long way toward articulating the latter.

The second might be equivalent to the stance of the Buddha, who had to go into the city of temptation and sin before he could be fit to be the Buddha. True simplicity, in this case, suggests a passage through something onto higher ground. This is the wise poem, convincing only if we sense everything in the poem feels like it's been discovered, not delivered from on high.

The not so good poem is written, perhaps on the same subject, by a person of different stature. Somebody's disciple, perhaps. Or a sensitive comrade instead of a profound one.

⚹

All poems are moral to the extent that they are evidence in content and form of an attentiveness to the details and circumstances of our lives. They get right the things they pay attention to, which always implies a correction of some sort. The issue is not right versus wrong. It's right versus off (the imprecise, the superficial, etc.).

The morality of the poet is to keep his/her tools sharp, always to be ready for the convergence of deep concern with subject matter. In this sense, craft and care for the integrity of language are the only things that separate the poet from the obvious moralist.

The not so good moral poem often works against some abuse or injustice and in its zeal gives content more attention than composition. This is the gift that falls apart, the one years later you can't seem to find when the giver comes to visit.

⚹

It is often tempting to conclude that in a good poem the poet has taken large risks. But risk is rarely the right word. Ambition is more precise. Some poets, formally or otherwise, are more ambitious with their material than others are, but they are more likely thinking about how to do justice to that material than about going out on a limb. The success of a good poem is linked to its necessity, to a subject that presents itself to the poet with a particular urgency. And the methods itself to the poet with a particular urgency. And the methods and devices employed by the poet arise out of the same necessity: the gestalt of subject and craft. (Of course in politically sensitive or totalitarian countries certain subject matter involves true risk, the risk of publishing the necessary poem.)

Interestingly, the not so good poet in Western countries often takes more risks than does the good poet. Superior craft and talent lessen the likelihood of falling on your face. In basketball, for example, it's common to hear that the very good player wants the ball at the end of the game, wants to take the crucial shot. This is not bravery, but confidence, and a kind of obligation. The not so good player is likely to shoot too hard or soft, or just inaccurately. Nevertheless, it is sometimes necessary for the not so good player to take the big shot. This should be applauded at the time, regardless of the result. In the long run, though, all that matters is true accomplishment, not one very good shot but many, some of them memorable.

Basketball and Poetry:
The Two Richies

BASKETBALL WAS MY FIRST LOVE. OR PERHAPS IT WAS MY RELIGION, if religion can be defined as that which most governs your life. As a teenager, I played almost every day, sometimes shoveling snow off the schoolyard court in order to do so. Sometimes I played in the dark, a distant streetlight the only illumination. If there was no one to play with I played by myself, imagining opponents or just practicing my shots. By the time I was fourteen I was five feet eleven, and the only freshman to make the varsity high school team. But I remember the coach looking at my small feet and shaking his head. "You're not going to get any bigger," he said, and he was right. I set about cultivating skills appropriate to someone my size. Shooting. Ball-handling. And I *thought* basketball when I wasn't playing it.

Since my mid-twenties, I've written and thought poetry that way, a lover's way, at odd hours, my whole self, or as much of myself as I could bring to the task, involved. "Play for mortal stakes," Robert Frost called it. And often it is a kind of serious play, play that brings one closer to self and reality, and thus is not always pleasurable. Basketball, on the other hand, served to delay my entry into the real world, which of course was part of why I loved it.

I think that if it hadn't been for Richie Swartz and Butch van Breda Kolff's decision to play him instead of me as the shooting guard on the 1960 Hofstra College basketball team, I might have been able to delay such entry indefinitely. But after a good sophomore year in which I was the team's second-highest scorer, Richie Swartz showed up and began for me a two-year lesson, often humiliating, about limits. Richie Swartz was good, pure and simple. But basketball is a game of relativities; the correct word is "better." Swartz was better than I. From the first time we covered each other in practice this was evident. He could block my jump shot. He could steal the ball from me. The writing, as they say, was on the wall, and it wasn't poetry.

If basketball offers you the possibility of transcendence, it more regularly offers you a sense of your limitations, though the two are sometimes intertwined. Every opponent presents to you a different set of latitudes or confinements. But basketball is a team game, and a good coach and good teammates can make use of your limitations, even free you from annoying defenders. No one could free me from Richie Swartz. Richie Swartz turned me inward to where doubts are, and doubts, while good for the poet, are bad for the athlete. In retrospect, Swartz turned me further toward the examined life, which, as everyone knows, is where angst resides. I accepted as fully as I did the existential literature I was reading at the time. It's only the fool who denies that his jump shot has been cleanly blocked, or that he's suddenly emptyhanded. You are what you do, and don't do. Worse, it was all so public. I didn't have any face-saving lies to tell. No, I had plenty. All transparent.

In basketball it's common to play with people better than you. To grow up on the schoolyards in Queens was to know something about hierarchy and pecking orders. I had sought out good players because they were the yardsticks by which I could measure and sometimes exceed myself. But I had never before had to play every day against someone who so consistently prevented me from being effective, and that ineffectiveness carried over into game situations. Hesitant that entire year, 1960, I rarely played as well as I had the year before.

The equivalent in poetry writing would be not just to know, say, that Yeats is a great poet (obviously that's desirable), but to have the achievements of Yeats block your ability to write poetry every time you tried. The poets who keep writing do so in the face of such greatness; if they were reasonable, they'd stop. There's much to be said for obsessiveness and stubbornness. Poets need to be somewhat driven in order to push forward; talent isn't quite enough.

I didn't let Richie Swartz entirely defeat me. I just made some adjustments with how to live with my first love. There's always a Richie Swartz out there, antithesis to your thesis. As the poet Robert Hass wrote in an epigraph to his book *Praise*, "We asked the captain what course of action he proposed to take toward a beast, so large, so terrifying, and unpredictable. He hesitated to answer, and then said judiciously, 'I think I shall praise it.'" I may not have been as judicious as that captain, but Swartz was a formidable player and good for the team. I cheered him from the bench, my heart healing a little each day.

But it was basketball with and without Richie Swartz that I had in mind when I began this, especially basketball's élan and its connection to writing poetry. As a former jump shooter with some ability, I remember what it was like to "get in a rhythm," to become "unstoppable," that feeling that the ball could not help but go in because you had entered the realm of magic, a place that was both yours and beyond you. I have a clear memory, even though the event took place over thirty years ago, of the evening I scored 45 points. I was a few years out of college, and I was playing in the *Long Island Press* League, which had teams composed of players like me, a combination of has-beens and almost-beens—a decent league, we used to think. I still see the box score as it appeared in the *Press* the next day. Dunn: 20 field goals, 5 foul shots, 45 points. I often had scored 20 points or so, but never before had I scored more than 40. I missed very few shots that night and was aided by a childhood friend, a teammate, another Richie, who recognized early that some kind of magic was occurring. He passed the ball to me at exactly the right moments in exactly the right places (*my* places) on the court. Such an evening wouldn't have happened without him. I could liken him now to my perfect reader, historically equipped and presently attuned to understand my best stuff. His name was Richie Goldstein. Henceforth to be known as the good Richie.

I tell this story not to brag about my prowess, though I admit to a certain pride in telling. I'm mostly interested in discussing what it means to be hot, those happy moments, to quote myself, when "practice and talent metamorphose / into a kind of ease." On that evening I was better than myself. Every previous hour on a basketball court, all my muscle memory, all my ability, converged that evening with dream. In fact I had dreamed, had visions, of such an evening. Every kid who's ever played has had such visions. "Unconscious," someone said afterward. "That guy was unconscious."

That I was. And long to be. Perhaps basketball and poetry have just a few things in common, but the most important is the possibility of transcendence. The opposite is labor. In writing, every writer knows when he or she is laboring to achieve an effect. You want to get from here to there, but find yourself willing it, forcing it. The equivalent in basketball is aiming your shot, a kind of strained and usually ineffective purposefulness. What you want to be is in some kind of flow, each next moment a discovery. Unconscious? Maybe, but more accurately a movement toward higher consciousness, of saying what you didn't know you could say, propelled by the mysteries of the process. The hot basketball player, however, has a distinct short-term advantage over the hot poet. He did it. Everybody knows he did it. The Nobel Committee need not meet to decide on it in private sessions. This is why scoring 45 points is more vivid in my memory than the writing and completion of any single poem. And why poets are often tormented. Yes, they might write successful, brilliant poems. But so few others agree or even care that they did. The fans don't stream into the studios and garrets.

I think every poet needs two Richies—one to come up against, the other to act as a muse. The tradition in all its forbidding excellence is what the serious poet engages, consciously or unconsciously, every time he or she sits down to write. It can be as seminal as it is daunting. To have had a Richie Swartz in my basketball life may have prepared me to score 45 points some years later. Certainly to have had the good Richie on that magical night was to have had an inspiriting agent—I almost said angel. "I did it myself." That's the comment of the poet insufficiently respectful of mystery, not to mention his forbears.

I've always been pleased, though not surprised, that so many of the best basketball players are intelligent. They understand the demands of a given situation, they do with their abilities what is necessary for the team, much as a good poet learns not to dazzle unless it contributes to the entire poem. Lesser poets and lesser basketball players never seem to learn that lesson. Not to pass the ball to the open man, for example, has many corollaries in poetry writing, all of them equally self-indulgent. To love a line too much because *you* wrote it, even though it doesn't work in the poem. Or to put in a poem something that happened to you, whether you've made a place for it or not.

It's lovely to watch a team yield to the temporary brilliance of a particular player. A good team will always adjust to someone with a hot hand, will know that it's in their interest to get the ball to that person, as Richie Goldstein did in my case. Similarly, a poem might have to expand to accommodate an important discovery. The poet's job always is to find a livable home for what he's found himself saying or doing. If he can't, he needs to save the wonderful discovery for another occasion, or abandon it entirely. "Court sense," basketball pundits called it. I know some poets who don't have it.

Wallace Stevens in his poem "On Modern Poetry" talks about "...sudden rightnesses, wholly / containing the mind, below which it cannot descend, / beyond which it has no will to rise." When the networks replay great moments such as Julius Irving's driving, swooping layup, or any of Michael Jordan's acrobatics, we have instances of sudden rightnesses, clearly recognizable. Announcers often loosely call these moments a kind of poetry, which may be accurate in the Stevens sense: utterly sufficient. But I worry about such locutions in our culture, which so often trivializes poetry. Too many poems are reduced by their readers to a single meaning, capsulized into catchphrases, distilled into information. Poetry's sudden rightness exists within larger contexts, and are right because of what precedes and follows them. They may be extractable, but at a cost. Here, basketball and its quick pleasures are part of a national problem: the short attention span, the quick, uncontemplative take. Poems are often demanding because they are trying to be equal to the complexities of the world and how it feels to be alive in it.

I've learned something about sudden rightnesses from basketball as well as from poetry. But poetry alone has slowed me down, taught me patience and the rewards of contemplation. There are reasons why people don't exchange high-fives in libraries. Poetry teaches you to say "yes" quietly — and at its best it doesn't let you escape from experience, from the hard business of living. To be a poetry fan you have to be prepared to wince, to have some of your shibboleths subverted. If you're a true fan, nothing again will ever be satisfactorily reduced to the thrill of victory, the agony of defeat. "Works of art," as Camus reminded us, "are not born in flashes of the imagination, but in daily fidelity."

Now I only play basketball when my brother comes to visit, two or three times a year. Out of old habit we get the ball, go to the schoolyard, and play one-on-one. He's fifty-eight, three years younger than I, and he almost always wins. Our abilities are so comic that we hold and bump a lot, and there's not a move that either of us has that the other hasn't seen a thousand times. "What to make of a diminished thing," Frost says. Indeed.

I like to think of Richie Swartz this way, maybe with a bum leg, fat, out on some schoolyard, just trying to keep something that was good and felt good intact. Who knows, maybe he hasn't lost a step, as Odysseus never does in rereadings. After all, he's Richie Swartz. Whatever his condition, something of his transcendent past must come back to him. Sweet moves and the ball in the hole; nothing like it. Well, almost nothing. It's something you don't forget, and with luck by the time you're fifty you've replaced it with something else, or can settle for the vicarious. Without luck…God knows, those old battlefield stories are legendary.

My brother and I play until we're exhausted, a stage soon reached. Each of us has usually made at least one shot that brings back a semblance of the old powers. Two such shots can create delusions of a major order. At dinner, we're likely to replay those moments. Our wives exchange the glances of grown-ups bemused by their children. But neither of them ever corkscrewed into the paint, double-clutched, and kissed the ball just right off the backboard.

⌘

Some Reflections on the Abstract
and the Wise

MOST OF US HAVE HEARD CAUTIONS ABOUT ABSTRACTION IN poems, about didacticism, the tendency to tell instead of show. We've correctly passed on these cautions to others, and have been aware of them as we composed. But more and more I've become aware of how many poems please me which violate these cautions, which risk being abstract and unabashedly "wise." I know that one person's wisdom is likely another's old baggage and this is one reason why attempts to offer it often fail. Still, I'd like to offer some speculations on the subject.

As we all know, we must please before we can instruct. Whether abstract or concrete, we want the language of the poem to be fresh, surprising. We want the poem's rhythms and sounds to authenticate its assertions. These are simply the basics. And there's no reason why they can't be operative in an abstract poem. That they are so often not operative frequently has to do with amateurism (lack of style, craft, and something to say) and sometimes with the difficulties inherent in direct statement.

"Wisdom lines," for example, get their bad name because more often than not half-poets, as Marianne Moore refers to them, use them. The result, she says, is not genuine. (At any given time, we can be sure that there are more half-poets than poets: thus the abundant evidence that one should avoid such direct handling of statement in a poem.) With wisdom lines, with any abstractions, we're usually in the presence of a conscious truth, one that we can readily get elsewhere or dispense with hearing it at all. Its context doesn't enrich or support it. We feel toward it as we feel toward a preacher who doesn't embody his sermon. It lacks the blood and bone of experience. It says "Love is…" and we are impelled to think of alternatives.

Williams's "No ideas but in things" is itself a wisdom line that insists such lines have no place in poetry. It was good advice when Williams wrote it, and, like most poets of my generation, I grew up with it as gospel. It was only in the act of writing, of discovering what I wanted to do or say in a poem, that I realized Williams's admonition was too narrow and exclusive. Though I don't wish to reduce this issue to two epigrammatic statements, I've come to hold Steven's definition of the imagination, "the power of the mind over the possibilities of things," as a valuable companion statement to the Williams quote. It suggests, among other things, that if we're working well we can create the contexts in which our discoveries and claims can be believably received. As I said, these two statements are companions: Stevens suggesting infinite latitudes; Williams giving us a proper caution. Because we're not looking for absolute truths in a poem, rather for something that can be believed, we must look for contexts to support our abstract statements.

Mostly, as any practitioner knows, it isn't "looking for," it's what we end up with and have to shape. One may surmise in the following excerpt that Donald Lawder wrote his poem out of a desire to instruct his student, Richard, and to provide us with a chance to overhear this instruction.

IN POETRY, EVERYTHING IS PERMITTED

> *For my student Richard who wrote*
> *"I'm horny tonight."*

Semantics
is dull stuff
but so's
your horniness
to the innocent
bystander.

To those of us
involved
seeking always
to involve others
in what involves us

only the meaning
of our meanings
is important.
Poetry is not
a happening.
Poetry

is what happens
when we permit
whatever happens
to happen.
It is this act
of permission

permitting even
the impermissible
to happen
that differentiates
poetry
from madness...

It's clear that this poem needs its epigraph and dedication so that the poem's otherwise preachy statements have an occasion, an excuse. The poem appears to be first for the "real" Richard and only secondarily for us, something we can enjoyably overhear without thinking that the poet is presuming we need such information. Too, the poem's recurrences are well-timed and give us something to listen to besides the message. In short, Lawder has written a poem, however didactic, that manages to please in many of the ways we want our poems to please.

To those of us
involved
seeking always
to involve others
in what involves us

is abstract yet clear and rhythmically sure. What's even more important is that it's a statement that makes us trust the author. He wants to speak to us, involve us in what he's involved in. As Roland Barthes wrote in his *The Pleasure of the Text*, "The text must prove to me that it desires me." Lawder is chiding the solipsistic Richard for being preoccupied

with his own horniness. It could have been loneliness or sadness or any-
thing the amateur writer tends to conceive as being peculiar to himself.
Lawder's poem indicates he's not going to make the same public error.

William Stafford, too, apparently risks saying straight out what he
means about his subject:

THE LITTLE WAYS THAT ENCOURAGE
GOOD FORTUNE

Wisdom is having things right in your life
and knowing why.
If you do not have things right in your life
you will be overwhelmed;
you may be heroic, but you will not be wise.
If you have things right in your life
but do not know why
you are just lucky, and you will not move
in the little ways that encourage good fortune.

The saddest are those not right in their lives
who are acting to make things right for others:
and that self will never be right:
no luck, no help, no wisdom.

On closer inspection, however, we notice "the right in your life" recur-
rences, the word "right" strung through the poem giving it its subtle
music. Which is to say this little essay of a poem is not prose. But what
really makes this overtly instructive poem successful? First and most im-
portant is that the poem articulates for us some things we've probably
half known and felt. It gives our inchoate knowledge shape and order,
and it's wise without suggesting that the author is interested in showing
off his wisdom. At the same time, it must be acknowledged that it's a
small poem whose truths are reductive. If the poem were any longer, it
would have needed to start working against itself. Clearly, one could
make a counter-case to each of Stafford's assertions. For example, we
can think of people who are troubled *and* wise. That's the problem with
abstract statement; it often makes us quarrelsome. If we don't trust the
voice, the statement can seem arbitrary, if not wrong.

Somehow this poem convinces us that it is more meditative than assertive, even though it is addressed to a vague you and is so absolutely sure of itself. How did Stafford get away with this? Maybe just because he is who he is, but a few further observations might be worthwhile. His narrow definition of wisdom — "wisdom is having things right in your life / and knowing why" — is only made palatable by what follows it. We learn the poet understands wisdom to be involved with "how one lives one's life." Wisdom, therefore, is something personal, not Delphic, not carved in stone. Wisdom is living well, and this homey, small truth takes some of the onus off the instructional nature of the poem. It's the "little" ways that encourage good fortune. The choice of "little" cooperates with the overall tact of the poem and further adds credibility to the voice. If there is a lack of complicity in the voice (usually a problem) it is compensated for by a kind of compassionate knowingness. One senses, as in certain abstract poems of Rilke's, that Stafford embodies the truths he's presenting, that these truths are more offerings than lessons. There's no doubt, in a craftsman's sense, that Stafford has learned "those little things that encourage good fortune." The poem is an embodiment of those little things, both wise and crafty, and finally confirms itself. Notice how dependent each line is on the others. The poem is an argument. It sways back and forth in its incremental way, modifying, extending, then collecting three crucial words from the text — luck, help, wisdom — and with concision and finality concluding its case. It exemplifies how direct statement can satisfy, but it also suggests the perils of abstraction. Readers who do not find these truths kindred have nothing sensory to compel them. They could easily become argumentative.

A poem that tries to be overtly wise about its subject but does not succeed is Douglas Crase's "Replevin." It was collected in his otherwise very fine book *The Revisionist*. It begins:

> If the beginning of love
> is loss, possessing it
> in places where you know
> it can be seen, then
> the reason for love is
> retrieval...

The poet starts off fairly well. Often the choice of "If" in a poem so de-
liberately didactic is smart one; it suggests that the poet is in the act of
weighing what he's going to say. But soon the trouble begins, and we be-
come too aware of the poem's mechanics and the poet's labor. With just
the small relief of a modifying claim, the poem continues:

> If the manner of love
> is displaying it, faithful
> as if belonging were,
> then the assumption of love
> is correcting it…

The poem moves in this manner all the way through. Its formal strategy
is built on a series of if-thens and is consistently *that* without variation
until the end. Because of the mechanical feel of the poem, I find myself
not trusting the poet on this subject. Yet there are some interesting wis-
dom lines. "The reason for love is / retrieval" is provocative. As is the
conclusion "…and the life / of love is embracing / its perpetual unat-
tainable selves." I like these lines, but I don't trust their speaker's me-
chanical voice. The poem's rhythms work against its assertions. It's dif-
ficult for us to believe that anything this singsongy could be sufficiently
contemplative. Instead of having "a meter-making argument," as Emer-
son says a poem should have, this poem is pushed along by its one
cadence. In fact, it's reasonable to assume that the poet got trapped by
his if-thens, that he might have allowed himself much more to say if he
allowed himself to depart from his one-note approach. The poem feels
unlived as a result.

Leonard Nathan wisely omitted "The Law" from his impressive *New
and Selected Poems*. It's a marriage poem, presumably about the diffi-
culties of faithfulness and unfaithfulness, and it begins promisingly.

> All around us things hold together
> by a tense balance of forces, the lonely
> negative side of one joined
> to the lonely negative side of another…

But Nathan never manages to give us any specifics about the marriage
in question. After several such lines, probably because they create nar-
rative expectations, I found myself thinking, "Tell me what's going on!"

The poem is complex in its phrasing, intelligent throughout, but the information in it is skeletal; we keep hoping for some narrative flesh. It lacks a context that would enable us to evaluate its claims.

Whereas Stafford's poem was unabashedly general, the you a generalized you, Nathan's poem is personal, written to a real you. Curiously, the Stafford poem seems more true to its subject and certainly less evasive. Perhaps I should say that, instead of personal, Nathan's poem is private. Only the addressee could know how most of the poem's assertions connect and inform. All we have to go on is, "So when I read your letter a third time / and it still said no, I finally saw / that marriages are made / in refusal…" Every other line in this two-stanza, fourteen-line poem is rigorously abstract. There are guesses we can make from the scant information we get, but I don't want to make up my own poem. It's Nathan's poem, and I want him to do more work for me.

"The Law" is just one of many poems that demonstrates the well-known pitfalls of abstract language. It is tempting to proffer some rules about the use of such language: that it's problematical when (1) the poem is private, (2) when the poem also has concrete language, but doesn't balance or pattern the two, and (3) when the poem suggests a narrative, then forsakes it for generalities. But these should be thought of as cautions rather than rules. The only rules that should be obeyed by poets are those they freely choose. Rules, like the constraints and boundaries imposed by forms, are usually invitations for poets to be ingenious.

William Bronk is arguably our best contemporary abstract poet. Over his long career, he's not wavered, no matter what the fashion, from his particular way of working. What saves Bronk is his relentless distrust of anything that might easily pass for the truth. In his most passionate ideational poems, he usefully distrusts his own mind, and certainly his own sentiments. Here's a poem that is typical of his style.

THE HOLDING

Of lovers, one senses how, coupled, their joy is to think
their singleness, together, to find themselves;
how, holding each other, they think to hold
as well as themselves, the truth, reality.

We honor their wanting; what better could we want than that?
Or, more than honor, we feel what they feel.
If not for another sense, then this were all:
we sense that what they hold is not the truth.

But it isn't wrong to want what they want.
If wrong is wrong, the wrong is not the want.
We sense that what they hold is not the truth.

How much of what we want — ourselves, the truth,
reality — is not for getting. What we hold
or how, no matter. What we hold is not the truth.

The poem is written from a distance, albeit an empathetic distance. It is nothing if not abstract. "What we hold is not the truth." It ends with this wisdom statement, yet one that arises, it seems, out of a lament. How good it would be if our loving constituted a truth, the poet is implying. But, alas, it doesn't, at least not one that can be held for long. The poem's "we" seems to include Bronk. It's not a royal "we." Perhaps one saving quality of an abstract poem is that it might suggest a dialectic; we trust that its truths are in the process of being modified, if not refuted. I don't hanker for specifics from "The Holding." It makes no narrative promise as the Nathan poem does.

Wendell Berry's "Marriage" is a poem that manages to combine the virtues of abstraction and direct statement while demonstrating that there are ways to engage the senses other than by concrete language. Here, as is evident in several of the poems under discussion, phrasal recurrences and repetition of words underscore and give emotional weight to the poem's assertions.

MARRIAGE

How hard it is for me, who lives
in the excitement of women
and have the desire for them
in my mouth like salt. Yet
you have taken me and quieted me.
You have been such light to me
that other women have been

your shadows. You come near me
with the nearness of sleep.
And yet I am not quiet.
It is to be broken. It is to be
torn open. It is not to be
reached and come to rest in
ever. I turn against you,
I break from you, I turn to you.
We hurt, and are hurt,
and have each other for healing.
It is healing. It is never whole.

Convincing rhythms, and the wisdom arrived at out of the personal. A fine balance of the specific and the general. In this poem there's a clear sense that the poet feels what he knows. The assertiveness in it tends not to make the reader argumentative. The first half of "Marriage" could be anybody's romantic poem, perhaps not unlike the first half of marriages. It's the insightful tough-mindedness of the second half, born out of affection and the pain of affection, that redeems the first half. It almost seems as if Berry sat down one day to write a love poem to his wife and worked through his conventional feelings about her and marriage until he arrived at the poem's first important truth: "It is to be broken," a truth that is poignant only because the tone, already established, is pro-marriage. (It is the absence of a demonstrable tone, among other things, that makes the Nathan and the Crase poems so difficult to appreciate.) It's no accident, since wisdom is usually something arrived at, something discovered *in process*, that the first wise lines occur in the middle of the poem. We are not inclined to call this poem didactic for much the same reasons we're not inclined to call the Stafford poem didactic. It seems as if the poet is discovering what he wants to say as he goes along, and though we know it's never quite that simple, the rhythms testify to the hard-won nature of these claims. Berry is conscious of both the personal and public nature of his subject. We sense that he's speaking to a specific person and, simultaneously, for all of us, exploring one of the mysteries of marriage.

William Carlos Williams, certainly not thought of as an abstract poet, was perhaps most affecting in "Asphodel, That Greeny Flower," that long didactic poem written to his wife when he was an old man. It is arguably his most moving poem, full of directly offered wisdom about love, most of it striking, some of it quite banal. I want to speculate on why a few of the passages in it are successes and why some of the language fails. A premise I'd like to begin with is that if a poem has created an emotional climate it can more easily get away with wisdom lines. Williams is well into Section I when he writes, "It is difficult to get the news from poems / yet many die miserably every day / for lack / of what is found there." This, I think satisfies out of context, yet in context it satisfies more. It follows a rather lengthy address to the woman, his wife. It's a celebration of her combined with an apologia for the speaker's shortcomings in their long marriage. A few lines before, the speaker said, "My heart rouses / thinking to bring you news / of something / that concerns you…" Thus, the wisdom lines come off of emotional language and are received by the reader both as lines which extend a sort of lament as well as present a clear and interesting truth. It is finally, perhaps, the built-in lament within the truth that makes the truth so touching. If these lines had occurred at the beginning of the poem we might have liked them anyway, they are so powerfully rendered, but I don't think we would have been as touched by them.

Section II of "Asphodel," however, begins this way:

> Approaching death,
>   as we think, the death of love,
>   no distinction
> any more suffices to differentiate
>   the particulars
>   place and condition
> with which we have been long
>   familiar.

I think these lines are rather poor and offer us some pointers on what not to do. They fail because not only are they didactic, but they succumb to the language of didacticism. Words like "distinction," "differentiate," "particulars," formal constructions such as "with which," are the dry ingredients of philosophical debate. I find the sense of these lines appealing; they convey a truth, but I'm not persuaded by the language to *care* about this truth at this moment in the poem. It's hard to pursue in a poem truths that don't first engage us with their surfaces. William's voice is full of authority in the first example and has almost none in the second. In the first he was in the act of discovering the language that was appropriate to the emotional occasion. In the second, after the first two lines, he offers what for him must have been a much more conscious truth, or so the rhythms and language would suggest.

Later in "Asphodel," Williams shows another way of handling "the wise statement" in a poem, by phrasing a statement as a question. "What power has love but forgiveness?" It's risky to ask such questions because most of us can think of several answers. But in context I think it works and serves to modulate what might have been preachy as a statement. The question allows its content to be implied and further allows the poet to register his doubt, which is useful. "What power has love but forgiveness?" begins a long section of the poem in which forgiveness connected with love is a motif, and we see the speaker exploring this question as he goes. If it had been phrased as a statement, such as "Love's power lies in forgiveness," it would have effectively ended exploration and the speaker would have been forced to move on to something else.

Another way of avoiding the didactic or at least avoiding being accused of it is to indicate what you're doing in the title, as if to say I know I'm not supposed to be doing this, but here it is, and I'm slightly apologizing for it. We see evidence of this in the plethora of "Instruction" or "How to" poems that are being written today. A particularly successful poem of this stripe is, "A Didactic Tale," by the Polish poet Tadeusz Rozewicz. It is subtitled "Rights & Duties."

> At one time I don't know when
> at one time I thought I had the right the duty
> to shout at the ploughman
> look look listen you blockhead
> Icarus is falling
> Icarus the son of vision is drowning
>
> leave your plough
> leave your land
> there Icarus is drowning
>
> Or that herder
> with his back turned to the drama
> of wings sun flight

fall
I said oh blind ones

But now I don't know just when
I know the ploughman ought to till the land
the shepherd watch over his flock
the venture of Icarus is not their venture
this is how it must end
and there is nothing
earth-shaking
about a beautiful ship sailing on
to its port of destination

TRANSLATED BY MAGNUS J. KRYNSKI
AND ROBERT A. MAGUIRE

I don't know if Rozewicz knew the Auden poem or even the Williams poem on the same subject, though he certainly was aware of the Breughel painting. The wisdom in this poem is about wisdom itself. It is, if you will, wise about wisdom just as Stafford's poem is, but is more self-questioning. It is also about learning humility and this helps modulate the didactic element in it. The conventional expectation for a poem of this type is for it to move from ignorance to sophistication, and this poem does that. The pleasing touch is that, in this case, sophistication is equated with becoming less sure of what one's rights and duties are. In the first part of the poem the speaker is full of conviction and moral outrage. In the second part he is perhaps equally sure of his convictions, but he's learned to respect the possible importance of the ordinary. He has more fully entered the world of multiplicity. Given the title, I think we are pleased that so little in this poem *is* didactic. Perhaps only in Wallace Stevens' poem "How to Live, What to Do," in which not a single word of advice is rendered, is a title resisted more.

Both Williams and Rozewicz are taking stock of their lives in these poems. Each has gained some perspective on something and wishes to tell us about it. Though the Williams poem, obviously, is more ambitious (clearly I haven't attempted to do it justice here), both poets were faced with the problem of how to keep such information active, dramatic. The danger inherent in poems like these is that the poet, already aware of his more mature perspective on a particular issue, will render it statically. If that happens, whatever wisdom the poem may contain seems as if it has come out of preformulated certainty. The poet seems self-satisfied, the poem didactic. But if the weighty parts of a poem are *in motion, in flow*, we more readily accept them. They feel part of the poem's drift and fabric.

I've saved William Meredith's poem "Crossing Over" for the last, because it satisfies most of the conditions I've been discussing.

CROSSING OVER

It was now early spring, and the river was swollen and turbulent; great cakes of floating ice were swinging heavily to and fro in the turbid waters. Owing to a peculiar form of the shore, on the Kentucky side, the land bending far out into the water, the ice had been lodged and detained in great quantities, and the narrow channel which swept round the bend was full of ice, piled one cake over an-other, thus forming a temporary barrier to the descending ice, which lodged, and formed a great undulating raft.... Eliza stood, for a moment, contemplating this unfavorable aspect of things.

> *Uncle Tom's Cabin*, CHAP. VII,
> "THE MOTHER'S STRUGGLE",
> HARRIET BEECHER STOWE

That's what love is like. The whole river
is melting. We skim along in great peril,

having to move faster than ice goes under
and still find foothold in the soft floe.

We are one another's floe. Each displaces the weight
of his own need. I am fat as a bloodhound,

hold me up. I won't hurt you. Though I bay,
I would swim with you on my back until the cold

seeped into my heart. We are committed, we
are going across this river willy-nilly.

No one, black or white, is free in Kentucky,
old gravity owns everybody. We're weighty.

I contemplate this unfavorable aspect of things.
Where is something solid? Only you and me.

Has anyone ever been to Ohio?
Do the people there stand firmly on icebergs?

Here all we have is love, a great undulating
raft, melting steadily. We go out on it

anyhow. I love you, I love this fool's walk.
The thing we have to learn is how to walk light.

Whereas the Stafford and Bronk poems largely speak ideationally, Meredith's voice resonates with emotion but maintains the kind of balance and evenness that's suitable to its subject. His is a mature, affectionate, intimate voice — not unlike Berry's — though this poem has more of a dramatic life than Berry's and a more compelling, metaphorical thread. The long, useful epigraph permits Meredith to play off material that would likely have been cumbersome in the body of the poem, and probably accounts, to some degree, for how clean and essential the poem is. He's able to begin with the utmost immediacy: "That's what love is like." The line seems narrow and assertive, but in fact we don't know yet what he means. The rest of the poem will be its illustration. "The whole river / is melting. We skim along in great peril..." is the beginning of the illustration, true enough as a comment on love, but not yet affecting because the reader is still unsure how Meredith is using the "we." It could be a generalized "we" at this point, which means the author would have great distance from his subject and be risking another kind of peril, the "on high" stance. When the poem becomes clearly personal — "I am fat as a bloodhound, / hold me up. I won't hurt you..." — Meredith has done a service to his earlier lines. When we reread them they have a greater emotional gravity and they work both personally and collectively. This is a lover's poem and, like the Lawder poem, it's written to a real someone. It's talking to the loved one about a victory of sorts: love is precarious and they still love each other, and the speaker knows a little something about why. Again, this wisdom is addressed to the lover, but of course we're meant to overhear it. Compare it to most love poems which attempt to affirm too easily or whine too privately, and we recognize the poem's achievement. The poem acknowledges that "old gravity owns everybody," which a lesser poet would let lie in all its solemnity. Meredith follows it with "We're weighty," a pun which lightens the moment and is reflective of the poem's emotional and intellectual balance.

"I contemplate this unfavorable aspect of things." Meredith *knows* the conditions of the world. He accepts them. Like Jake Barnes, he wants to know how to live with and in them. For a moment, though, he's going to allow himself a romantic indulgence.

Where is something solid. Only you and me.

But he's too smart to stop there. Later he writes, "Here all we have is love, a great undulating / raft, melting steadily." He's tough-minded again. They're in love and their love is in peril, not necessarily because of any particular problem, but because of the nature of love and the world in which one lives. The way of things. This tough-mindedness, this sagacity, permits the beautiful, affirmative ending: "The thing we have to learn is how to walk light." It is a poem that only could have been written by someone who has assimilated many loves, many failures, who knows "We go out on it anyhow" is both courage and, in a Sisyphean sense, all we can do. The wisdom line that concludes the poem satisfies because it arises inevitably and naturally out of what preceded it. Meredith established the sufficient emotional climate for it. And it's a small, modest truth, not abstract in its context, grounded in experience that we feel sure is behind the poem, though not necessarily in it. How does one learn to write a poem like this? One doesn't. One lives awhile, practices one's craft, waits for some convergence of subject, self, and talent.

As with love, so with writing. The perils exist, especially when we find ourselves inclined to being weighty and/or abstract. We have to learn how to walk light. Or, if we must have a graver tone, we must remember what walking light means: knowing enough about the conditions of our subject that we don't let its weight sink us, that in a poem we keep alive with our discoveries, our successful movements from one precarious moment to the next. Finally, we don't stop loving because of the difficulties. Nor do we eschew abstraction because of the inherent dangers.

Gambling:
Remembrances and Assertions

MY FATHER HAD A SMALL ROMANCE WITH DANGER. HE FOLLOWED
sirens, for one. Even if we were eating dinner, he'd get in his car and
pursue a police car or fire engine. And he was a gambler, though he was-
n't at the race track or the poker table when he lost everything.

In his early forties, he gave all the family savings, five thousand dol-
lars, to my grandfather (his father-in-law) to help pay the hospital bills
for grandfather's secret mistress. My grandfather died soon thereafter,
the debt unpaid. When my mother asked where the savings went, father
said, "the track," and lived with that lie for fourteen years until his own
death. He was thought of as a wastrel, and drank, I think, in order not
to speak. Nobility? Stupidity? I have my opinions, none of them certain.

Our family myth was that gambling destroyed my father and placed
us in a financial situation from which we never fully recovered. It had its
degree of truth. Though I know it was some blend of circumstance,
propriety, and male camaraderie that caused his downfall, a part of me
always has felt he made a gambler's decision when he loaned grand-
father that money. Even if he'd been paid back, there still would have
been a sizable period of time when he wouldn't have been able to ac-
count for the zeros in the bank book. Whatever else it may have been,
this was high stakes gambling.

I suppose if I were rational about my legacy, I'd play everything
straight. Yet I drift to the casinos on boring afternoons, sometimes un-
boring afternoons. I play in a weekly poker game. I love to handicap and
bet on the horses. And I continue to be fascinated with the various ways
in which one can ruin or vivify one's life.

In many ways, I may replicate my father's behavior, though I've never gone as far as he did. That is, past the balance that reasonable poker players maintain: where something higher (like nobility) or lower (like greed) could cast you into the abyss. To some degree I consider this a failure on my part. Great gambling may involve the uncommon next step.

Good high-stakes poker players are neither noble nor greedy. They've sized up their fellow players, know a good deal about probabilities and tendencies, and wish like poets that their most audacious moves are perceived as part of a series of credible gestures. In big stakes poker games, as A. Alvarez has pointed out, they need to think that the fifty thousand dollars they've raised, say, on four diamonds showing, is leverage, not money that might go toward a new house. To the extent that they translate money into commodities or security it's likely they'll give something away at crunch time. A hesitation. A tic. The great gamblers, and there are not many, don't need anything. They simply wish to prevail. And we know how dangerous people are who don't need anything. The purity of leverage. I raise you fifty thousand dollars. I'm saying I have a flush. I'm neither smiling nor shaking. See me if you dare.

I'm not that kind of gambler. I'm full of commonplace desire mixed with modest means. Though occasionally I've taken relatively large chances, I mostly think of gambling as fun, an evening's diversion. Worst of all, I do think of what money can buy. At crunch time, my astute poker-playing-friend says, I reveal something, though of course he won't tell me what. But I *am* calculating, I have some sense of when to push the action, when to withdraw. I only flirt with being my father.

Early on, though, the signs weren't good. One year after my father, drunk, told me his secret (it was unmistakably – the way pain is – true), I got into a neighborhood card game. Acey-deucy, a game that requires only boldness, no skill. I was seventeen, working as a check-out boy at Food Fair earning very little money, and I had with me only thirty-dollars. The pot kept increasing. It was my turn; the two cards dealt were a king and a three. I could bet any portion of the pot, wagering on the probability that the next card would fall in between those two cards. I'd been counting the cards already played. The odds were immensely in my favor. I told the other players I didn't have the money, but could get it if I lost. The pot was $216: I called it. The next card was a three. It was my grandmother to whom I appealed, who lovingly gave me the money. Our secret, in a family of secrets. It took the entire school year to pay her back.

This was my introduction to gambler's guilt, carried around in silence. For days after, I'd look at my mother to see if she knew. No, grandmother didn't tell her. I felt that strange mixture of relief and desire-to-be-punished, a sensation which gamblers experience when their concealments are successful. Paying back grandmother was a kind of punishment, but the privacy of our pact kept guilt from tripping over into shame. I lived in limbo, a somewhat livable place.

Such gambling failures didn't occur often. Neither did such titillations. I learned more intimately than ever that there's a relationship between heartbeat and pleasure, heartbeat and fear. Around this time I met a girl who became my girlfriend, a different kind of rush. She slowed me down, taught me new options for free time. Lady luck.

⚙

Some things I know: If you go to the casino with one hundred dollars, don't expect to win a thousand. If you approach poetry writing without reading great poetry, you will reach, at best, the level of your ignorance.

⚙

When to be bold? A gambler's question, to be sure. But perhaps an important question for everyone. The gambler's sense of it is instructive. You go on what you know and can intuit. A mixture of knowledge and daring. The fool knows little and thinks he knows more. The great gambler knows something about himself, and everything about his territory. I was once in a poker game with Donald Justice, a very good player. In seven card stud he had two jacks showing, and even though no one raised him, he folded. He was happy to say why. The likelihood was that he'd end up with two pair, jacks-up, and jacks-up seldom won in seven card stud. A measured decision. A measured poet, one of our best. Yet one imagines someone like Walt Whitman thinking "Jacks-up, Jesus

Christ, I'd risk America on that." If you're not a Walt Whitman, you end up in debtor's prison.

It's wiser for some people to be bolder than others. It's often a matter of temperament, secondarily a matter of nerve, and somewhat a matter, to borrow William Matthews's phrase, of the degree to which we can "metabolize loss." Good gamblers trust their ability to correctly read situations, yet what one *does* with what he knows and feels is what separates one gambler from another. Great gamblers trust their knowledge *and* possess the equipoise necessary to go out on that edge where the gods and demons live. Failure lives out there on that edge. So does luck, and a sensation that's richer than satisfaction, though not as sufficient. I wish I could say I've been there more often.

Short of the edge, there are different, quieter pleasures. The banter and table-talk at friendly poker games. The arc and sway of luck over a long evening, and all the little moves one must keep to himself. Or a good Black Jack table, everyone playing smart, all rooting against the dealer. And the dealer, if he or she has personality, rooting for the table. Every gambler could extend this list according to the game and its niceties.

※

A nicety: The Racing Form — that poor man's anthology of histories, equine and human — provides the kind of information that instructs us about the insufficiency of certain knowledge. Yet, I've always been pleased by the talk, gambler's talk, that emanates from such information. I especially love the talk about why a particular horse can't lose. When that horse loses we're left sometimes with pure intelligence, a fine mind that we've been privileged to overhear, however wrong.

※

Several years ago I went to Vegas to meet a childhood friend, the kid picked on for being clumsy and boorish. He was now a pyschotherapist in Los Angeles. I'd kept in touch with him for twenty years, through many difficulties. I was the last remnant of his humiliating childhood, and he needed to remind me of that every time we saw each other, usually through some perverse behavior.

We met at the Stardust Hotel. It was 1979. He was stoned when I arrived, wearing buckskin from shoulder to foot. This allowed him to make fun of my sports jacket, professorial, conservative. I let him get away with it, out of guilt, I suppose. I, too, had picked on him when we were kids.

He wanted to leave The Stardust and go to Circus-Circus. In the carnival-like area above the gaming tables he knew there was a test-your-accuracy basketball game, a difficult one — a very small hoop and a regular sized basketball. He said he wanted to win a prize for his son. You had to make three out of three to win a prize. Stoned as he was, he was able to make three out of three a few times. The best I managed was two out of three. He collected some prize coupons, not enough to win the giant stuffed bear he desired. *Many* coupons were needed for that. Next we went to the break-the-balloon-with-the-dart game, where he proceeded to fail. But we'd come to Vegas to gamble, and I guess he decided to start. He leapt over the counter, a 40 year old pyschotherapist with a 40 year old poet sidekick, grabbed all the coupons from the waist of the girl in charge, said "Let's run, let's get out of here," and we ran like the criminals we were while she screamed for Security.

He had given me no choice, and I was furious with him as we ran. I was also terrified, could see jail and ruin ahead of me, or a bullet in the back. Somehow, we got away. Safely in our room at The Stardust we laughed for what seemed like hours. When we stopped I told him I thought he was crazy, and if he kept doing things like this we couldn't be friends. He was not apologetic. It would be two years and one other aberration later before I fully got the message.

That next morning, different shift, different personnel, we returned to Circus-Circus and he got that bear. We did gamble at the tables that weekend, won a little, lost a little, but there was no doubt about what had been the real gambling.

Clearly, he had been a dumb gambler, and I a not wholly unwitting pal to self-destructiveness. The stakes were much too high, the reward not worth the risk. That we got away with it is often the spur that sends bad gamblers back to the original scene: the primal success. Such gamblers always are in pursuit of the once-achieved giant stuffed bear. The metaphorical police are frequently waiting.

It's interesting to note that probably an old wound was at the heart of my friend's actions. It pushed him out of conventional behavior, led him to the giant stuffed bear. Driven-ness. The poet in me took note of it.

※

When I'm served a plate and the server says, "This is very hot, don't touch it," I always touch it. Just a tap with one finger, a quick with-drawal. I love how my wife shakes her head when I do this. It's sure-thing gambling. No chance of getting burned, and an audience that pre-tends to believe otherwise.

※

I still remember the horse's name, Dancer. Dancer in the Fifth at Aque-duct. My father had gotten a tip that Dancer, a first-time starter, had been training exceptionally well and was a lock. There was even a hint that a fix was in. I'm not sure how old I was at the time, fifteen or six-teen. I'm only sure that it was before father gave all our money to grand-father, and before acey-deucy, because nothing needed to be concealed. He announced in the morning he had a tip and was going to Aqueduct, just eight miles from our house. I told several of my friends who in turn told their fathers. There must have been twelve of us, true-believers, easy-money Algers, American down to the depths of our dreams, who went that day.

The inside word must have gotten out. Dancer went off at 6-1, though there was nothing visible in The Racing Form to warrant such betting support. My father was still happy with the possible payoff. He bet $100, a lot of money for him, for us. It was a six-furlong race, a sprint. Dancer broke from the gate so fast he had a five length lead in the first furlong. He led all the way until the stretch when every other horse, the swift and the untouted, passed him.

There's a moment in a race when you know your horse isn't going to win. Dancer started to go backwards, or so it seemed. In fact, "going backwards" is a familiar description for a horse that starts to fade. "C'mon Dancer," which we'd been screaming, was replaced by "Shit" and "Goddamn" (heavy accent on last syllable), and then silence. Eleven of us looked at my father. He had that smile you often see on gamblers' faces, part resignation, part bemusement that once again the sure thing wasn't. "It was a good tip," he said, by which he meant that the horse showed speed and *was* ready, albeit for a three-furlong race instead of a six. "It'll be interesting to see what he does next time," my father said. Already, he was metabolizing loss, getting beyond it.

A gambler, like a good hitter in baseball, knows he'll fail more than succeed, even though he expects to succeed each time in the singular instance. A part of him is prepared for loss. Thus, the gambler's smile.

If other aspects of our lives — our love life, our work life — are satisfactory, we can manage to live with loss. However, when our lives are going bad or have gone bad, that's when the demons rise up and won't be appeased. Dostoyevsky perhaps was the first to suggest that the gambler, by which he meant the compulsive gambler, secretly wishes to lose. The demons, as in D.H. Lawrence's "The Rocking-Horse Winner," are always demonically chanting "more." The compulsive gambler wants something like love or quiescence, and in his best moments only gets money. He wants to fill some emptiness, and he pushes his bets so far he ends up with a greater emptiness, perhaps an emptiness that has an odd measure of solace in it: he can delude himself that he knows its source.

After my father became known as a wastrel, after he lost respect at home, he lost that gambler's smile forever.

⁂

Some things I know: When I've had a fight with my wife, walked out of the house and gone to the casino, I've always lost. I stay too long, could be one explanation. More likely I'm seeking to deepen my mood, to let sullenness feed on sullenness, to enter that cocoon state of the wronged where everything corroborates misery. The needy person should never gamble. The needy person wants to.

⁂

Sports gamblers (basketball, football) are an especially needy breed, and I'm happy to say I've never been one of them. Usually they are the gamblers who require regular or even constant action – the bulemics of bettors – perpetuating a cycle of fullness (new bets) then emptiness (wins *or* losses). There's never closure.

Robert Frost felt that without theme you wouldn't be able to properly slow down a poem. Certainly you wouldn't know where to end it. Theme could be a synonym for having a center, a place both nourishing and nourishable. The sports bettor, more than most gamblers I know, has no such place.

The opposite of these bettors is the fan, the lover (*ama*teur), who finds a sufficiency in the game itself and/or in the performance of one particular team. In the middle are the fans who, now and then, for fun, wager with friends that their favorite team will win. Those people, of course, you can bear to be around.

But sport's bettors depress me. Often they're like the kind of stock market players openly pleased when General Motors streamlines operations by laying off thousands. They talk point spreads instead of people, cumulative points (among two teams) instead of, say, a player's excellence or brilliance. I've heard them cheer when a quarterback has been injured. At their best, values aside, they're too fidgety to savor a fine moment. And they're not capable of the gambler's smile.

Clearly, I reveal my prejudices here, and one should know when he's become moralistic that he has little more to say on his subject. I should admit that all of us who gamble are, importantly, fellow gamblers. Perhaps the ones I've criticized didn't have, way back when it counted, a lucky grandmother or girlfriend or, for that matter, an unlucky father who was an emblem of decency. A small turn here or there, and I could be them.

My resolution for the New Year is to work on my soul. I used to think that first you had to locate it, but now believe it makes itself invisibly palpable when it's been tended to. I wish there was more talk about soul. We've largely given up such talk, in favor of commerce, politics, the talk of people who expect answers, results. I've said in a poem, "the normal condition of the soul is to be starved." If this is true, those of us who are vigilant about our souls are trying to feed them. *Save* them? Faust gambled with his soul, which suggests that we should be using different currency when we gamble. But it seems to me that gambling, at its healthiest, is one way of activating the soul, nudging it from its hungry sleep. I'm speaking about gambling in its most reductive form: taking a chance. The *act* of taking a chance is energizing. The *art* of the act of taking a chance can lead to the sublime. Like the time I saw Paco Camino exhibit perfect grace—a series of slow, exact moves—with an erratic bull in Madrid. Or Miles Davis, years ago at a club, riding an impulse beyond himself. Surely those folks who play their lives and their work eminently safe don't often put themselves in the position where they can be startled or enlarged. Don't put themselves near enough to the realm of the unknown where discovery resides, and joy has been rumored to appear. The realm of the unknown is contiguous to the realm of failure. The gambler, deep down, has made a pact with failure. He'll accept it because it has interesting neighbors. In such realms the soul, I think, is fed, not to mention exercised.

But those of us who gamble for pleasure mostly know more level moments. The small loss, or win. The perfect bluff that when successful precludes joy because the satisfaction must be kept to oneself. (Here some of us know the virtues of suppression). Or the breaking even. I suspect that the spouses of gamblers have heard "I broke even" more than any other lie. To literally break even, of course, isn't bad. If we love to gamble it means we've had some free entertainment. But only the existentially terrified *play* to break even. Aren't we after what dailiness seldom provides: the edge? We're betting we're smart and talented and/or lucky enough to lean but not to fall. Sometimes we are.

☷

Complaint, Complicity, Outrage
and Composition

To complain, protest, register outrage, are familiar impulses in most of our lives. And what occurs in our lives inevitably is reflected in poetry. Yet Robert Frost wrote that "grievances are a form of impatience," and went on to say he didn't like them in poetry. He preferred "griefs." Yeats told us that quarrels with others produce rhetoric. Poetry came out of quarrels with oneself. They were responding to bad poetry that has been written out of such impulses. They knew if we are too wedded to ideas or impulses that got us started in a poem, there's a good chance we won't discover very much. And not to make discoveries in a poem can lead us to, among other things, writing position statements. Such statements always arrive with inherent limitations we struggle to get beyond. An authentic sense of complicity helps. A general and habitual resistance to our own certainties is also useful.

In this regard, two words come to mind, both with mixed reputations and in a sense opposed to each other: inspiration and strategy. Inspiration is a word that over the centuries has needed to be debunked, redefined, or defended. For example, Poe's "Philosophy of Composition" was written to demonstrate that nothing as breathy as inspiration produced "The Raven." It's an essay which suggests that a proper strategy is considerably more important. Fernando Pessoa wrote, "I feel beliefs which I do not hold. I am ravished by passions I repudiate." Inspiration? Yes, but with fictive implications. Wordworth's phrase "emotion recollected in tranquility" posits a middle ground; while composing, we recall how we felt about something, and this can lead to "the spontaneous overflow of powerful feelings." The poet presumably has enough distance to be both emoter and strategist. Of course we know that poets find inspiration in less emotional sources, say in "the power of the mind over the possibilities of things," as Stevens did. But poems of complaint most often suggest direct inspiration and earnestness of purpose. Poems of outrage always do.

Three premises: (1) "Strategy" can suggest that poems are written the way battle plans are made, that all we have to do is calculate some correct angle of attack and we'll have ourselves a poem. Good poems don't get made that way. What appears to be strategy is usually no more than the poet seeking and finding a form that will determine matters of emphasis and the rate and intervals of disclosure. Often it's the poet responding to the demands and limitations of the poem's language, rhythm, and content. There may be an overt strategic approach to the material at the poem's outset, as in a persona poem or as in a Jarrell poem that I'll discuss later on, but after that initial decision, a willed strategy won't accomplish much.

(2) Inspiration can just as easily occur in the act of composition as it can be engendered by a preceding event. A poem's first discovered moment may be its most seminal, and we know that words in conjunction with other words can be sexy, propulsive. But however inspiration might occur, I think it's essential. It's a word we shouldn't be embarrassed to use. And it doesn't obviate having a strategy.

(3) Most poets know that what Yeats said is likely true, and therefore know how important complicity is in a poem that quarrels with others. But if we decide to be complicitous as opposed to feeling complicitous, most likely that will be apparent in the poem. What matters, of course, is that our poems arise out of genuine concerns and preoccupations, or that we discover those concerns and preoccupations as our poems evolve. Those of us who do not feel complicitous in the ills of the world always will be quarreling with others. Yet, as I will attempt to argue, some quarrels can be handled so successfully that we won't mind their lack of complicity, nor will we accuse them of being rhetorical.

I want to start with two complaint poems about men, written by women, one which has a compositional strategy and a degree of complicity, the other which has neither. First the latter, written by Penelope Scambly Schott.

MEN CAN LEAVE

They can put on their hats
like pure invisibility,
men can. Or shake this lamplight
off their shoulders. When they walk
out the door, the knob
doesn't freeze to their palms.

Nope, they march right out
under one moon or another —
its all the same to them,
leaving. A man doesn't care
about sunlight mounting a wall
or that pine smell under the steps.
Their shoeprints point one way:
Out. And never double back.
Not the gateposts mute in snow
or the planet under the boots —
nothing reminds men to weep.
They still believe they have choices,

men do.

The success of such a poem would usually depend on the insight-fulness of its claims in conjunction with credibility of the speaker. But since Schott makes no efforts to create a trustworthy or untrustworthy (my preference, in this case) speaker, the poem must survive on the claims that it makes. And it can't because of its absolutism. The male equivalent of this poem would be something called "Women Always Leave Sensitively." All women. Written with irony and contempt. There's no inclination on Schott's part to modify or refine a single claim. The poem is written out of a certain moral superiority. Many of the poem's claims, if narrowed or modulated, could be persuasive, or persuasive enough. For example, let's say the poem were called "He Can Leave," and was written about a specific man. The poem still wouldn't be complicitous or empathetic, but it would be more credible. Or say it had one or two that attempted to be sympathetic to the way some men leave, which indicated an awareness that men grieve in their leaving,

too. Wouldn't that strengthen the poems complaints? Wouldn't we trust
the speaker more?

What is absent is a compositional strategy which could make this
poem work. It is absent because the author in her single-mindedness
didn't think one was necessary. She thought she could tell the "truth."
Men most likely do leave differently than women do. But this poem con-
vinces me only that Schott is angry, and in her anger insufficiently in-
terested in the complexities of her subject.

Marge Piercy's poem "The Friend" is equally angry, but it has a clear
compositional strategy.

THE FRIEND

We sat across the table.
he said, cut off your hands.
they are always poking at things.
they might touch me.
I said yes.

Food grew cold on the table.
he said, burn your body.
it is not clean and smells like sex.
it rubs my mind sore.
I said yes.

I love you, I said.
That's very nice, he said
I like to be loved,
that makes me happy.
Have you cut off your hands yet?

In contrast with the Schott poem, it has two immediate virtues. One,
its title is usefully narrower, and two, the poem's indictments are made
dramatically rather than assertively. With its great economy, it delivers to
us not only the sadistic male but his masochistic partner, each an exag-
geration of a type. We sense that one couldn't exist very well without the
other. We're sure that a maker is behind this poem, someone who has
digested certain experiences and reduced them to their essentials and
infused them with tone. The man, of course, is most severely indicted,

but who can help but laugh (snicker might be more accurate) at the way he's presented, laugh, really, in the recognition of how well he's been isolated and caught. The poem may have a grievance behind it, but it isn't a position statement. It asks for our assent compositionally; that is, by its arrangement of details and with its hyperbolic ironies.

William Meredith seems to me masterly in how he manages the poetic complaint. Here is his poem written to Nixon in 1969 at the time of the Cambodia bombings.

A MILD-SPOKEN CITIZEN FINALLY WRITES TO THE WHITE HOUSE

Please read this letter when you are alone.
Don't be afraid to listen to what may change you,
I am urging on you only what I myself have done.

In the first place, I respect the office, although one night
last spring, when you had committed (in my eyes)
criminal folly, and there was a toast to you, I wouldn't rise.

A man's mistakes (if I may lecture you), his worst acts,
aren't out of character, as he'd like to think,
are not put on him by power or stress or too much to drink,

but simply a worse self he consents to be. Thus
there is no mistaking you. I marvel that there's
so much disrespect for a man just being himself, being his errors.

"I never met a worse man than myself,"
Thoreau said. When we're our best selves, we can all
afford to say that. Self-respect is best when marginal.

And when the office of the presidency will again
accommodate that remark, it may be held by better men
than you or me. Meantime, I hear there is music in your house,

your women wear queens' wear, though winds howl outside,
and I say, that's all right, the man should have some ease,
but does anyone say to your face who you really are?

No, they say Mr. President, while any young person
feels free to call me *voter, believer,* even *causer.*
And if I were also a pray-er, a man given to praying,

(I'm often in fact careless about great things, like you)
and I wanted to pray for your office, as in fact I do,
the words that would come to me would more likely be

god change you than *god bless the presidency.*
I would pray, *God cause the President to change.*
As I myself have been changed, first my head, then my heart,

so that I no longer pretend that I don't swindle or kill
when there is swindling and killing on my nation's part.
Well. Go out into your upstairs hall tonight with this letter.

Generous ghosts must walk that house at night,
carrying draughts of the Republic like cold water
to a man parched after too much talk and wine and smoke.

Hear them. They are elected ghosts, though some will be radicals
and all may want to tell you things you will not like.
It will seem dark in the carpeted hall, despite the night-lights

in the dull sconces. Make the guard let you pass.
"If you are the president," a shade with a water-glass
will ask you (and this is all I ask), calling you by name,

himself perhaps a famous name, "If you are the President,
and things in the land have come to all this shame,
why don't you try something new? This building rose,

laborious as a dream, to house one character:
man trusting man anew. That's who each tenant is
or an impostor, as some of us have been.

Meredith takes great pains to establish the modesty of the speaker
and his complicitous sensibility: "I am urging on you only what I myself
have done." He even risks the danger of making him wise:

A man's mistakes (if I may lecture), his worst acts,
aren't out of character, as he'd like to think,

> are not put on him by power or stress too much to drink,

> but are simply a worse self he consents to be.

If we're not trusting the speaker by now, we never will. The intent of this letter/poem is to criticize and to give advice, but Meredith knows that no one listens very well to a raised voice, or to obvious insults. One of his most adroit touches in this poem of complaint is

> ... Meantime, I hear there is a music in your house,

> your women wear queens' wear, though winds howl outside,
> and I say, that's all right, the man should have some ease...

Given the climate of the times and the bombast that occurred in a good deal of poetry written then, Meredith's stance in this poem is that much more remarkable. Of course, the powers-to-be didn't listen to the quiet, measured voice any more than they did to the bombastic ones. But the issue for us as poets is not that our poems lead to immediate political or social change. It's that with our poems, with all the choices we make in them — diction, tone, arrangement of details — we are in the act of conferring value on experience, we are suggesting little (and sometimes big) degrees of importance. This poem measures a particular experience and a particular man. Because it is a made poem, not just an utterance, it can be read with pleasure long after the historical occasion that spurred it, as can, say, Yeats' "Easter, 1916."

Meredith's poem has a clear and sly strategy of presentation, though we can as easily say that it seems to have arisen out of a series of strongly held convictions in search of the right contextual language. When Meredith says, for example, "I'm often in fact careless about great things, like you," I'm aware that this is an argumentative strategy, but he makes me believe the admission as well. The poem confers value by trusting a sensibility that is dramatically antithetical to the one it's criticizing.

Yet it very well may be argued that Meredith's complicity is temperamental, so much part of his humility that it doesn't represent a discovery for him, that it pre-existed the poem so that he didn't learn about it in the act of writing. In this sense the poem is a performance, a finely modulated example of narrative tact.

In Seamus Heaney's "Punishment," on the other hand, we have a poem in which the speaker, and perhaps the poet, seems to find his level of complicity as he works his subject.

PUNISHMENT

I can feel the tug
of the halter at the nape
of her neck, the wind
on her naked front.

It blows her nipples
to amber beads,
it shakes the frail rigging
of her ribs.

I can see her drowned
body in the bog,
the weighing stone,
the floating rods and boughs.

Under which at first
she was a barked sapling
that is dug up
oak-bone, brain-firkin:

her shaved head
like a stubble of black corn,
her blindfold a soiled bandage,
her noose a ring

to store
the memories of love.
Little adulteress,
before they punished you

you were flaxen-haired,
undernourished, and your
tar-black face was beautiful.
My poor scapegoat,

> I almost love you
> but would have cast, I know,
> the stones of silence.
> I am the voyeur
>
> of your brain's exposed
> and darkened combs,
> your muscles' webbing
> and all your numbered bones:
>
> I who have stood dumb
> when your betraying sisters,
> cauled in tar,
> wept by the railings,
>
> who would connive
> in civilized outrage
> yet understand the exact
> and tribal, intimate revenge.

The poem begins with empathy "I can feel the tug…" and continues with precise observation about the woman's "punishment," humiliation, and death. Mid-poem, we learn she was an adulteress whom "they" punished, the "they" separating the speaker from the perpetrators. The first turn occurs with

> My poor scapegoat,
> I almost love you
> and would have cast, I know,
> the stones of silence.

Here, with its Christian allusion to "Let he who is without sin cast the first stone," Heaney has offered us both a self-criticism and a self-aggrandizement. He wouldn't have done anything to stop the punishment, but he also wouldn't have participated in it, having at least imagined or committed such a crime himself. This is a complicated moment, at once complicitous and differentiating. The self-criticism deepens in the next few lines.

> I am the artful voyeur

of your brain's exposed
and darkened combs...

Heaney's poem is successful because it has two turns. In the second turn he acknowledges that he understands the tribal response to the adulteress, suggesting that she was a citizen of a small town with a rigorous moral code. Most writers in poems of this length don't allow themselves two turns, but the first, in Heaney's judgment, must have been insufficiently true to the poem's emotional ambiguity. His quest for veracity pushed him toward the poem's unexpected discovery, and engaged complicity's impulse. It would be wrong to call these turns "technique" or "strategy." They are inseparable from Heaney's relentless examination of subject.

Complicity can be equated with truthfulness in this case, and impotence equated with imagination. The artful voyeur understands too much to act; he can empathize with the woman, he can empathize with the punishers. The poem is a paradigm of the writer's dilemma of having imaginative empathy with all sides, and Heaney to his credit gives each side its due. The tribal revenge, though, is "intimate," and the speaker who "almost" loved the woman and has been the "voyeur" of her death is seemingly envious of such intimacy. Heaney allows us multiple layers of complicity in this poem.

Sometimes it's possible to register complaint in poetry without complicity. Look at this poem by Theodore Roethke.

DOLOR

I have known the inexorable sadness of pencils,
Neat in their boxes, dolor of pad and paper-weight,
All the misery of manila folders and mucilage,
Desolation in an immaculate public places,
Lonely reception room, lavatory, switchboard,
The unalterable pathos of basin and pitcher,
Ritual of multigraph, paper-clip, comma,
Endless duplication of lives and objects.
And I have seen dust from the walls of institutions,
Finer than flour, alive, more dangerous than silica,
Sift, almost invisible, through long afternoons of tedium,
Dropping a fine film on nails and delicate eyebrows,
Glazing the pale hair, the duplicate gray standard faces.

There's a small degree of complicity here, beginning with "I have known" and continued with "I have seen." The speaker is intimate with the problem. But he's not part of the problem; if he ever was, he's no longer one of "the duplicate gray standard faces." Why does the poem work so well? We admire the poem for its sheer virtuosity, language finding language. The details collect into a portrait of what is a commonplace "industrial of institutional monotony and conformity" yet such tedium is rendered with verve. The haunting extended "dust" image that concludes the poem almost presages the link between asbestos and cancer, and, indeed, Roethke is suggesting a kind of workplace cancer, albeit a psychological one. Moreover, we sense the poem is a lament, and his tone permits Roethke to register his complaint without superiority. If we don't feel the lament, then the poem is just another condemnation. Lament is a form of understanding; it implies closeness to the thing lamented. It is complicity's good sister. In "Dolor" Roethke manages his complaint by focusing almost entirely on subject. He does not ask us to be terribly concerned about the role of the "I." If part of Meredith's success was in a sensibility that was antithetical to the one he was criticizing, Roethke's achievement resides in vivifying language and rhythms as he describes monotony.

But what about the poem of outrage in which the narrator is clearly divorced from the crimes he's describing? These are the most difficult poems to write. We know what we're outraged by, whether it be rape or the Vietnam War, and we're likely to reach the end of our thinking and feeling too easily. Most poems of outrage are too earnest to do anything but say what the author knew before the poem began. They're preformulated. Or they're just screaming. They rarely take us by surprise.

One poem of outrage which succeeds is Randall Jarrell's Holocaust fable.

PROTOCOLS

Birkenau, Odessa; the children speak alternately.

We went there on the train. They had big barges that they towed,
We stood up, there were so many I was squashed.
There was a smoke-stack, then they made me wash.
It was a factory, I think. My mother held me up
And I could see the ship that made the smoke.

When I was tired my mother carried me.
She said, "Don't be afraid." But I was only tired.
Where we went there is no more Odessa.
They had water in a pipe — like rain, but hot;
The water there is deeper than the world

And I was tired and fell in in my sleep
And the water drank me. That is what I think.
And I said to my mother, "Now I'm washed and dried,"
My mother hugged me, and it smelled like hay
And that is how you die. And that is how you die.

In "Protocols" Jarrell counts on his audience knowing the nature of this subject. Poets who consciously write political poems often actually think they're bringing us news that war is hell, racism is evil, etc. Jarrell's strategy in letting the children speak without perspective or fear makes the horror, if this is possible, more horrific. This is the act of an empathetic imagination whose impulses are as literary as they are moral. Jarrell's imaginative burden was to find language and rhythms that would approximate the confusion the children felt with the machinery of death and the familiar but desperate warmth of their mothers. The poem's storylike repetitions and half-rhymes, its metaphors ("I could see the ship that made the smoke"), all the literary devices serve to enhance the feeling of innocence. That is the poem's greatest risk: to make a "beautiful" construct out of material that is heinous.

This is a made poem, a transformation of outrage, rather than outrage pure. The orchestration of the voices is what breaks our hearts, more than the voices themselves.

It is one thing to write a poem of outrage out of empathy, another to write it out of direct experience. Paul Celan, a Rumanian by birth, saw his parents murdered by the Nazis, and he was sent to a labor camp. Is it more difficult to write a successful poem about horror one has experienced than about horror one has read about or observed? I'm not sure it matters. All good poems are victories over something.

FUGUE OF DEATH

Black milk of daybreak we drink it at nightfall
we drink it at noon in the morning we drink it at night

drink it and drink it
we are digging a grave in the sky it is ample to lie there
A man in the house he plays with the serpents he writes
he writes when the night falls to Germany your golden hair
       Margarete
he writes it and walks from the house the stars glitter he
       whistles his dogs up
he whistles his Jews out and orders a grave to be dug in the
       earth
he commands us strike up for the dance

Black milk of daybreak we drink you at night
we drink in the mornings at noon we drink you at nightfall
drink you and drink you
A man in the house plays with the serpents he writes
he writes when the night falls to Germany your golden hair
       Margarete
Your ashen hair Shulamith we are digging a grave in the sky
       it is ample to lie there

He shouts stab deeper in earth you there and you others you
       sing and you play
he grabs at the iron in his belt and swings it and blue are his
       eyes
stab deeper your spades you there and you others play on
       for the dancing

Black milk of daybreak we drink you at nightfall
we drink you at noon in the mornings we drink you at
       nightfall
drink you and drink you
a man in the house your golden hair Margarete
your ashen heir Shulamith he plays with the serpents

He shouts play sweeter death's music death comes as a
       master from Germany
he shouts stroke darker the strings and as smoke you shall
       climb to the sky
then you'll have a grave in the clouds it is ample to lie there

Black milk of daybreak we drink you at night
we drink you at noon death comes as a master from Germany

we drink you at nightfall and morning we drink you and
     drink you
a master from Germany death comes with eyes that are blue
with a bullet of lead he will hit in the mark he will hit you
a man in the house your golden hair Margarete
he hunts us down with his dogs in the sky he gives us a
     grave
he plays with serpents and dreams death comes as a
     master from Germany
your golden hair Margarete
your ashen hair Shulamith.

TRANSLATED BY CHRISTOPHER MIDDLETON

We don't have to know Celan's biography to appreciate the poem's
genuineness and power. It, too, is a transformation of outrage. Celan has
used music, specifically the fugue, to distract himself into poetry, to pre-
vent himself from simply crying out. Within the fugal variations we get
enough narrative to piece together a story. And the elegiac address to
Margarete and Shulamith makes specific and personal the outrage and
the lament. It is a "we" poem; the speaker is part of the victimization.
We do not expect complicity in that voice. The poem and its subject,
perhaps, transcends complicity, but Celan's poetic burden requires him
still to move beyond the predictabilities of his subject.

This he does in several ways. Where Jarrell used the conventions of
children's stories, Celan uses the startling figure of "Black milk of day-
break" and the polyphony of the fugue to insist that that milk gets drunk
over and over at all times of the day and night, and that this "horror" is
a kind of "dance" to the serpent man. Celan isn't attempting to teach us
anything new about the Holocaust. The poem aspires to song, and it is
indeed a song of sorrow. The repetitions and the slight variations from
movement to movement are as thematic as they are musical. Outrage
and grief, by the end, have found a form. It is form, an insistence and a
holding in, which takes the poem beyond the predictable.

If we're not (as poets) going to be complicitous in what we find
wrong and abhorrent, then we had better find ways to measure and eval-
uate experience that uniquely draw more attention to the subject than
to ourselves. If we are going to draw attention to ourselves (or some

surrogate "I" that speaks our poems) then we must remember we are characters in our own poems, part of the poem's fiction, and the good reader expects characters to be shaped by the author. This, or course, is the most difficult thing for beginning poets to understand. It precedes complicity, and leads to it.

A poem by C.K. Williams illustrates my point.

THE GAS STATION

This is before I'd read Nietzsche. Before Kant or
    Kierkegaard, even before Whitman or Yeats.
I don't think there were three words in my head yet. I
    knew, perhaps, that I should suffer,
I can remember I almost cried for this or for that, nothing
    special, nothing to speak of.
Probably I was mad with grief for the loss of my
    childhood, but I wouldn't have known that.
It's dawn. A gas station. Route twenty-two. I remember
    exactly: route twenty-two curved,
there was a squat, striped concrete divider they'd put in
    after a plague of collisions.
The gas station? Texaco, Esso — I don't know. They were
    just words anyway then, just what their signs said.
I wouldn't have understood the first thing about
    monopoly or imperialist or oppression.
It's dawn. It's so late. Even then, when I was never tired,
    I'm just holding on.
Slumped on my friend's shoulder, I watch the relentless,
    wordless misery of the route twenty-two sky
that seems to be filming my face with a grainy oil I keep
    trying to rub off or in.
Why are we here? Because one of my friends, in the men's
    room over there, has blue balls.
He has to jerk off. I don't know what that means, "blue
    balls," or why he has to do that —
it must be important to have to stop here after this long
    night, but I don't ask.
I'm just trying, I think, to keep my head as empty as I can
    for as long as I can.
One of my other friends is asleep. He's so ugly, his mouth
    hanging, slack and wet.

Another – I'll never see this one again – stares from the
        window as though he were frightened.
Here's what we've done. We were in Times Square, a
        pimp found us, corralled us, led us somewhere,
down a dark street, another dark street, up dark stairs,
        dark hall, dark apartment,
where his whore, his girl or his wife or his mother for all I
        know dragged herself from her sleep,
propped herself on an elbow, gazed into the dark hall and
        agreed, for two dollars each, to take care of us.
Take care of us. Some of the words that come through me
        now seem to stay, to hook in.
My friend in the bathroom is taking so long. The filthy sky
        must be starting to lighten.
It took me a long time, too, with the woman, I mean. Did I
        mention that she, the woman, the whore or mother,
was having her time and all she would deign do was to
        blow us? Did I say that? Deign? Blow?
What a joy, though, the idea was in those days. Blown!
        What a thing to tell the next day.
She only deigned, though, no more. She was like a
        machine. When I lift her back to me now,
there's nothing there but that dark, curly head, working, a
        machine, up and down, and now,
Freud, Marx, Fathers, tell me, what am I, doing this, telling
        this, on her, on myself,
hammering it down, cementing it, sealing it in, but a
        machine, too? *Why am I doing this?*
I still haven't read Augustine. I don't understand
        Chomsky that well. Should I?
My friend at last comes back. Maybe the right words were
        there all along. *Complicity. Wonder.*
How pure we were then, before Rimbaud, before Blake.
        Grace. Love. Take care of us. Please.

In many respects this is a most unpromising poem. Not many poems could survive Nietzsche, Kierkegaard, and Kant in their first line. How many more could say "blue balls," "jerk off," and "blow," and still be successful, even delicate, as I think "The Gas Station" is?

Williams's poem is not quite a quarrel with itself. The scene and the acts described are deliberately and necessarily tawdry; the speaker is reexamining his participation in them. He's speaking to himself, "hammering it down"; he's speaking to his intellectual and spiritual fathers; he's speaking to us. The poem is artful in its story of preconsciousness or pre-self-consciousness, yet the poem focuses on consciousness and its burdens. The "I" is very much a character in the poem, someone measuring the innocent vulgarity of a past experience against the present need to tell about it, to tell the story on himself. Why is he telling the story? That's the poem's and the poet's discovery. Complicity. Wonder. Both. In experience. And outside experience. Our amazing simultaneous capacities. The orchestration of the poem — Williams's ability to mix exposition with just the right amount of examination of that exposition — is commensurate with the phenomena it's describing.

One of the pleasures of this poem resides in how Williams resists and redeems the words he uses. "Take care of us" at the end, following "Grace. Love," resounds beautifully and ironically off of the earlier "Take care of us" associated with the whore. There's little possibility of grace without tawdriness and ugliness. And love is that much more meaningful when we've experienced those cheap, those rote, imitations of it. Williams's poem reminds us of this. His juxtaposition of pretentious "deign" and vulgar "blow" makes a resonant equation between words the poet wishes to speak in his poem's innocence and wants to criticize at the same time.

This stance toward experience, a dramatized complicity, permits Williams to present and evaluate experience, and to examine a consciousness in the act of presenting and evaluating. To be complicitous is to acknowledge being part of, but interestingly it also seems to be a distancing device, allowing Williams in this case to stand back, reflect, measure.

In this sense complicity is related to composition. We might say that this mind is constantly seeking to discover the extent of its involvement in what it's describing. It is always concerned with limits. Williams's expansive line is appropriate in that it, too, is seeking its limits. In every line Williams seems to test just how much he can flirt with prose and still write poetry.

In any of these poems we could speculate on the varieties of inspiration which spurred them, though I think, it's safe to say that the linguistic discoveries in the act of composition were at least as inspiriting as the events or attitudes which preceded them. This constitutes, then, a kind of double inspiration.

Can we say that in most poems, but perhaps especially in poems of complaint and outrage, there must occur this double inspiration? And that the demands of form might be a third kind of inspiration? In Celan's poem, for example, the initial inspiration came from outside the poem, the Holocaust itself. But it can be argued, I think, that the phrase "Black milk of daybreak" gave the poet something else to be propelled by and to live up to, that phrase "found" as many next moments as the engendering subject did. And surely the structural and rhythmical device of the fugue, once started, was equally propulsive for Celan, while also providing the pressure and titillation of limits.

In most of the poems under discussion a similar case can be made. When Williams wrote "Take care of us," its resonances beyond the literal clearly inspired him to take the poem where he did. Williams probably knew something in advance about the story he was about to tell, but he didn't know he was going to say "Take care of us," which turned out to be a kind of refrain, and thematically seminal. Locate a poem's first real discovery, and often you will find its motor, if not its ignition key.

But of course no one moment or effect makes a poem. When a poet sits down to write, it's useful (to paraphrase Faulkner) for the human heart to be in conflict with itself, and/or with something outside of it. Ideally, the two will exist in combination. After that, the mysteries of composition begin. That we are able to say a few things about those mysteries is like speaking about evolution without solving the problem of the existence of God. The mystery remains.

⚏

A History of My Silence

THERE WAS A YOUNG MAN IN MY POETRY CLASS WITH THE DOUBLE burden of having a terrible stutter and an imagination. He not only spoke with great difficulty, but his poetry demonstrated that he had a gift for intuiting what others might be feeling and thinking about him. Matthew spoke anyway. That was his bravery. But there was another thing about Matthew. He sang in the college chorus. When he sang he was all sailboats and wind; his stutter disappeared. That was his magic and his pleasure.

I taught myself to wait, no matter how long it took, until Matthew finished his sentences. It was a gesture to myself, to the muted boy in me, as importantly selfish as therapy. Every sentence Matthew finished was a victory for both of us. I did not tell him this. When he wrote, how pleased he must have been that one word immediately followed another.

As a boy and as a young man, I had none of Matthew's gumption in the face of my admittedly lesser problem: shyness. If a teacher asked me a question, I would say "I don't know" rather than say the answer I often knew. When required to give a speech in front of the class, I would stand there silently, turning red. Eventually, my teachers would give up on me, wouldn't call my name. I was grateful. My report cards were littered with C's, except in 7th Grade when Mr. Zenner gave me A's in all my courses. At the parent-teacher's conference, he explained to my astounded father, "Stephen is one of the best third basemen I've ever seen at his age." Mr. Zenner felt there was eloquence in sports. He must have thought my hand-eye coordination was a kind of overall accomplishment, perhaps a different form of speech.

It got worse, or, as some might think, better. At home, my mother would congratulate me on how smart I was. "Look how well he does in school," she'd say to my grandmother after observing five or six C's, and she meant it. School was what my family hadn't been good at. I, however, knew what being good at school meant. I knew what my friends Alan and Judy could do, not to mention Martin Propper. Martin Propper, the best student in both grade and high school, with the paradigmatic name. My speechlessness had something to do with knowing what a Martin Propper was. "Just be yourself," my father counseled. Bad advice when your self is some undefined creature between newt and dream-tiger. I would keep my self to myself.

In 1953 I turned fourteen, entered high school, and started to read books more serious than *Chip Hilton: Sports Hero*. My inner life began to collect its own comrades. There were no books in our house, however, on a permanent basis. We didn't even have a bookshelf, no less a library. But my maternal grandfather (who in fact lived with us and owned the house) regularly borrowed a novel from the small lending library at the pharmacy. He had arthritis, and every night with a bottle of gin next to his big chair he read and drank himself to sleep. He was the grandfather who had told me stories after dinner when I was a young boy. As a sailor in the merchant marine, a *Jewish* sailor (one of my favorite oxymorons), he had seen much of the world. He'd been around New York, too, as a theatrical agent. My mother called him self-educated. It was this grandfather who told me about books.

What a pleasure reading was: the world received in silence, at my own pace. I loved such a one-sided dialogue, the writer speaking to me who had nothing to do but take in. I dreamt and worried and exulted. I read all the Maugham books, and especially loved *Of Human Bondage*. Ah, that club foot, that hindrance. And Holden Caulfield, the bad student with the seismographic shit-detector, spotting the phonies. And in *Crime and Punishment*, Dostoyevsky—who would become my favorite writer—delineating a marginal man who lived inside his head with his ideas, deciding to become a man of action, superior to the mores of society. This was a delusion I found attractive. Books were about one's secret life! The more I read the more my world bifurcated. There was the Ozzie & Harriet world, in which I thought I should be living, where everything one thought was mentionable *out loud*. Then there was the shaded and shady and sometimes absurd world of un-mentionables, which books talked about, and which monologist Jean Shepherd addressed five nights a week at 10 PM on WOR, a show I never missed. Shepherd talked about familial inanities, forays into other neighborhoods, the things kids did in their hideaways, the kindred mysteries of his Indiana childhood. He gave childhood a voice, a drama; listening to him it was possible to believe that I wasn't strange, or, if I were, I had a good companion. But none of my friends listened to Shepherd. My father called his program "trash."

The bifurcation was exacerbated by the fact that we lived in the Jewish section of Forest Hills, New York, and I was being being raised as a Catholic in a household comprised of a Jew (grandfather), a Protestant (grandmother), a Catholic (father), and a Hybrid (mother). I had one gentile friend, Alan Arcuri. That's how we were referred to: the gentiles, the very sound of it suggestive of a lesser species. Everyone else I knew was Jewish. I went to dances at the Synagogue, but never asked anyone to dance. I played ball at the Jewish Center. I didn't date a non-Jewish girl until I was twenty-two. I was a Sunday Catholic, most Sundays anyway.

We didn't have ambivalence or doubt in our family. We merely lacked conviction. My mother converted to Catholicism eleven years after her marriage promise to do so. Though she put up a good front, always she seemed to have her fingers crossed when she admonished me about my Catholic duties. And I needed to be admonished. I missed Sunday mass. I'd been known to take the Lord's name in vain. I was Confirmed, while longing for the lavishness of a Bar Mitzvah, the gifts and the fun. My father went to church every Sunday, but there was something matter-of-fact about the way he recited the prayers when I sat next to him in the pew. He was thinking of something else.

I suppose it wasn't surprising that I never wholly believed what I was taught in catechism, or that I wasn't afraid of hell. The Catholic things: well, they weren't Jewish enough. Confession provided me with early training as a fictionist. If I'd been too good, I made up some bad things for the priest's sake. If I'd actually committed some venials or mortals, I omitted a few to avoid serious penance. It seemed like a game. I envied my Jewish friends their clear sense of historical victimization, their different sense of sin. But I spoke to no one of this. Such heretical feelings

seemed to have no proper outlet; they became another layer of my si-
lence. At age seventeen, when I told my father I was no longer going to
church, he threw a tirade that lasted, off and on, for two weeks. After
that, he never went to church again. I had liberated both of us.

My father was a vacuum cleaner salesman, affably Irish, unlettered.
My mother a housewife, half Jewish, half-Scottish, beautiful and warm
and simple, her life and looks limited by a heart condition that began
when she was thirty eight. During my high school years, my parents
lived together estranged. Typically, as dinner time approached and my
father wasn't present, my mother would call The Fleet Street Inn to ask
if Charlie was there. The bartender would say no. Ten minutes later my
father would arrive home. Or, he wouldn't, and I'd be sent on my bike
to fetch him. Always he was happy to see me, would buy me a coke and
introduce me to his friends (even if I'd been introduced before), and I
saw that his significant, affective life existed there. It was hard to get him
to leave. By the time we got home my mother would be doubly angry,
but she'd make dinner for him anyway, as if dinner, no matter what its
tone, was a link to a civility she needed to preserve. Because I knew my
father's secret, which was really grandfather's secret, and knew how it
was profoundly connected to his nobility, I could never get mad at him.
He had given all the family savings to grandfather to help pay the hos-
pital bills for grandfather's mistress, and, when confronted, said he lost
the money at the track. He was sparing the women, spearing himself.
He never told the truth, except to me. I knew too much. When he and
mother would argue, I'd just go to my room.

What happened at home seemed to corroborate what I experienced
in books: people had secrets and secret lives. Some circumstances of
our lives were beyond our control. Conclusion: Learn to be cool. Many
years later, in an elegy for my father, I would write:

> Nights he'd come home drunk
> mother would cook his food
> and there'd be silence.
> Thus, for years, I thought
> all arguments were silent
> and this is why silence
> is what I arm myself with
> and silence is what I hate...

> I carry silence with me
> the way others carry snapshots
> of loved ones. I offer it
> and wait for a response…

What's remarkable during those years is that I felt loved by both of my parents. Theirs had been a good marriage until their early forties, and perhaps they had developed sufficiently good habits of loving me, which they were able to carry forward. Yet how difficult it must have been for them—sullen together any evening my father drank, which was increasingly every evening, to manifest such care for me. They were proud that I was an athlete. And they'd tell me I'd be good at anything I wanted to be, even though there was considerable evidence to the contrary. Everyone should be the beneficiary of those benign untruths that make the possible possible. My self-doubts, my buck teeth and braces, my quietness itself, all had some beneficent warmth to live in. Love seemed more achievable than speech.

To this day, I wear my poker face. I have a history of letting you know only what is useful for me to let you know. Grief, heartbreak—it may be invidious to say that the shy, self-conscious person welcomes such things, but a part of me always is pleased to be startled out of myself into large feeling, to be moved to genuine, unmitigated speech. Or, in the rarer experience of ecstasy, to be moved to genuine silence.

Mr. Zenner was right. I was a good athlete. But I was better at basketball than at third base, yet no other teacher thought I deserved an A for such eloquence. This became very clear in high school where, academically, I just scraped by. I made the varsity basketball team in my freshman year and learned that in some circles action could satisfactorily substitute for speech. (I would learn later—after basketball—that I was crippled in the way that good athletes often are; I had few social gifts, didn't know how to initiate friendships.) Yet I was surprised, even back then, how bad I was at the banter my teammates seemed so naturally good at. In response to their good-natured joking and boasting, I merely smiled. From their locker room talk, I turned away, embarrassed. The adjective publicly used for me was "quiet." It really meant odd.

I remember feeling especially powerless. Other people—teachers, parents, certainly my stronger peers—controlled the terms and conditions of my life. There was no philosophy behind my silence, no Gandhi-like rigor. What resources do the languageless have? The tantrum? The sulk? The knowing smile? The smirk? I wasn't even good at those. Mostly my silence had shame in it, and impotence. I would have rebelled if I'd been sure the enemy wasn't myself. Over the years I've observed rage (that superior form of the tantrum) in others, and it seems like the province of those who've come to realize their silence was systemic, part of a larger oppression, a societal voicelessness rather than a quietness. I didn't qualify for rage.

I'm writing this from, in a relative sense, the vantage of the powerful. I have now a modicum of control over the normal superficialities of dailiness, and I know this is no small thing. Now when I'm silent it often seems to have the weight of choice behind it. In another sense it has America behind it, the entire history of American male silence, which only recently has come to be seriously analyzed. The strong silent type, the Frontiersman, the adventurer, those Gary Coopers of our mythic past, offer to white American males the permission to be silent. As long as a man is conventionally strong, the culture validates his silence.

I recognize this and consider myself among the questionably privileged. We now know that the notion of the mythic American male hurts its aspirants as much as it may help them. It protects them from the messiness of emotional attachments, thereby freeing them for action and accomplishment. Their god is progress, the god who dazzles and moves on. But back then I was an athlete. Also I was shy. The Marlboro man – rugged, intrepid – was calling to me. So was something or someone as yet undefined. I experienced the ambivalence that comes from having figured out that the hero to whom I half-subscribed had a bit of a social problem. How does one become like my student Matthew and fight through his awareness? I saw the images on the billboards and in the movies. Meanwhile, during the last two years of high school, I read books that took me into a complicated elsewhere. All of Hesse. *Look Homeward Angel* and *You Can't Go Home Again. Jude The Obscure.* And soon there would be Hemingway's Jake, a male hero I understood, appealing and damaged.

In college, still never speaking in class, I took a Fiction Writing course in which, incidentally, Francis Ford Coppola was the best student. He wasn't quiet at all. I had a small facility, and received some small praise, but wasn't very good at writing stories. Nevertheless I loved words, having hoarded so many for so long, and took pleasure in using them. Occasionally I loved them too much, like the time I used "alacrity" – a word I had just learned – three times in a very short story. Next to the third "alacrity" the professor wrote in the margin, "I know you know this word." I'd been caught, and felt that twinge of embarrassment I've come to understand is a good sign. There's hope for someone who can be embarrassed by poor word choice.

Though I was interested in my courses, I'd come to college primarily to play basketball. Two incidents, both on basketball road trips, stand out as crucial junctures in my history of silence.

The first took place in a hotel room in Scranton, Pennsylvania with two other Hostra players, Sam Toperoff and Dick Pulaski. Both were older than the typical undergraduate by four or five years. They'd been in the Army, were keenly and crudely intelligent, the best conversationalists on the team. Sam was an English major, Dick was majoring in Philosophy. It was 1959. I was a sophomore, a pure shooter, and I can't remember why I was in their room. Did they invite me? Did I just come by? They were talking about *Moby Dick*, the feel of it, good and mostly evil, the whiteness of the whale. It was unlike any discussion I'd ever heard in a class. It was about themselves, about obsession, the difficulties of being a good man, and it was occasionally funny. It was possible to be funny about serious things! I was sitting on the floor, listening. They didn't expect me to participate. The conversation went on almost two hours, and I knew it was the best talk I'd ever heard, knew that in my dream-life I wanted to know that much, be able to speak like that.

It was just possible that part of the reason they kept the conversation going for so long was because of me. Since both of them ended up being teachers, this might have been some early practice. Sam Toperoff became a writer as well as a teacher, and one of my enduring friends. For years I tried to equal his articulateness, his maverick tough-mindedness, his ability to make a room full of people his.

The other incident took place two years later. I was a senior. Sam and Dick had graduated. The team was in Gettysburg to play Gettysburg College. All twelve of us had gone to the movies to see Arthur Miller's

The Misfits. I was a solid member of the team, my teammates and I happily sharing a common vocabulary of crossover dribbles, pump fakes, bounce passes. There was nuance in such discourse, however limited. I was still bad at locker room talk, still alienated when naked people snapped towels at each other. I was taking a historiography course and had been stunned that history was attitudinal, philosophical, that historical truth was qualifiable. I was astounded that I didn't know this before. My intellectual life may have begun, and I was sitting in a movie theater with eleven other jocks watching a movie that I found fascinating. Afterwards we walked out into the sunlight. Ted, our center, the one we would go to at crucial moments in the game, asked me to explain the movie to him. The other ten players seconded his request. I hadn't known they thought of me as anything but Radar, the quiet guy, the good jump shooter. I explained it to them. I opened my mouth and the words came out.

In 1965, four years out of college, working as a copywriter in New York and living in Greenwich Village, I was invited by Sam Toperoff to play in a regular Sunday morning Artists & Writers schoolyard basketball game. I was trying to write fiction in the evenings, more for reasons of self-respect than out of serious aspiration, but I was invited because I could play. It was unlike any schoolyard basketball in which I'd ever found myself—competitive, yet polite, exceedingly honest. The players confessed when they stepped out of bounds as if they'd spent the previous night reading moral philosophy, they apologized when they fouled you, they caught you if you were in danger of falling. It was nothing like the New York playground fierceness I'd been used to.

Calvin Trillin was one of the players, Gerald Jonas another. Both were young writers at *The New Yorker.* Christopher Lehmann-Haupt was just starting to review books for the *Times*; he was there, too. Toperoff had just won an *Atlantic* First prize for a short story, and his first novel had been accepted. Everyone, even the ones whose names are now not recognizable, was attractively quirky, interesting.

After the games, we bought Seven-Up and Mission Orange and went to Trillin's nearby apartment in the Village to cool down, but mostly to talk. Trillin, as he has now demonstrated to the world, was a great raconteur. So was Toperoff. It was high wit by men in sneakers, the

Algonquin revisited, just a little sweatier and further west. The conversation was rangy — books and people and basketball — and, what I didn't know you could talk about, talk itself.

At the end of the first year of Sundays, we rented the upstairs room of a Greek restaurant in the West Forties, had a mock awards banquet, wives and girlfriends included. "Most Improved Jewish Ballplayer" was one of the awards. Someone won "Highest Jumping White Man." I received "The Ringer" Award for the player unfairly brought in with outside credentials. When I went up to the mike to accept, I couldn't think of a single witty thing to say. I said "Thank you." It was inexcusable. All the others paid homage to their long suffering mothers, gave credit to the flag, to the booze that kept them healthy.

Artists & Writers Sunday basketball went on for two years, as did the talks in Trillin's apartment. I didn't speak more than a few words the entire time. I was conscious of listening, storing up, pleased to be part of it. It was my Black Mountain College. At night I told my wife everything I could remember — the best lines, the liveliest stories. I discovered I had a knack for recollection, for isolating the representative details. It must have come from all of those years of listening to Jean Shepherd.

The history of my silence would be a lie if I didn't admit that I could talk to women before I could talk in groups. One-to-one, the kind of talk that first arises out of sex, *sotto voce*, is eased by the body's ease, that wordless declaration of worthiness transmitted skin to skin, which leads to larger and larger verbal permission. It's the permission that love (more than just sex) gives, the language of sweet nothings, *play*; I suppose that one is never so un-selfconscious as when one is playing. It's the language — play-language — with which I've always been most comfortable. The bed as playing field. Breasts as a kind of post-coital lounge area where nothing is too silly or too intimate to be said. If a man can speak intimately, can get off his white horse for a few moments, perhaps even *likes* being off that horse, most women will offer him all the latitudes of speech that he might need. If also *he* can listen, it's likely — other things being equal — that he's entered the realm of what intelligent women consider truly sexy.

But here's where the problem for the man starts. When intimacy begins so does concealment. Some partition of the heart closes as another slides open. Is this true only for men? I doubt it. One thinks of something one shouldn't be thinking and must withhold from the loved one. It could be as simple as I don't like the way she laughs at the end of her sentences. Even though her sentences are wonderful! Or, I love her, but also I am attracted to x. At the heart of such concealments is silence. If one has a history of silence, the withholding might go unnoticed, at least for a while. If one is a novice, it's likely he's going to speak about his withholdings out of guilt and ruin everything, as the congenitally honest do. At any rate, girls, women, have for me been the progenitors of my greatest verbosity and my greatest silence. I would tell them everything. When I got to know them intimately I would tell them less.

If the Muse is female and a man is visited by his Muse and has learned to tap the stored-up resources of his silence, he learns and yearns to tell her more. All on his terms (though this may be his ultimate delusion). Clearly, once again, I'm speaking about the options of the powerfully silent. I've known such options on a few occasions – heady, seductive; verbal lilac wine. But my powerful, controlling silence, at best, has brought only short term rewards. Finally, nobody wants it. It's a taker, a self-protector. The true lover wants to give everything away. This is why a writer should never be expected to be a true lover. The writer, shortly after great love, uses. I would think this would also be true of the writer trapped in his powerlessness, though then the using is perhaps more excusable.

One might say, because my mother was so affirming, that I've sought out nurturing women like her. This is certainly true of the woman I chose to marry. Emotional generosity – I like it more than I deserve it. Things grow from it, the penis being one of them. I don't mean this as a joke. When one gets beyond middle age, he should understand just how important such generosity is. Worry about sexual performance is one of the things about which men are most silent. The silence of the lambs, we who have been educated to be wolves.

Most women are prepared to understand the varieties of male silence, as long as the silence isn't aggressive or remote. Perhaps women truly disposed to men always are seeking to know if there is any vulnerability in our silence. The best women want to know if there is any quality in it.

My wife does not believe in my shyness, or in the years of discomforting silence, which I've told her about. From the beginning, her affection for me and her belief that I was smart gave me permission to speak. I spoke. I was even bold. She allowed me to appear as if I knew what I was doing and saying.

But the history of any marriage involves accumulated silences. Withholdings. When particular withholdings become intolerable, they of course provoke fights, arguments. Or, if one is a certain kind of poet, poems. Or all of the above. Contrary to current psychobabble, a marriage that is working well permits certain silences. Silence is an aspect of freedom. Aren't people who live in despotic countries often forced to speak? Maybe my wife's greatest gift to me, given that she doesn't believe in my history of silence, has been that she tacitly acknowledges and accepts that I withhold things from her. I try to act accordingly for her. It's always, though, a matter of balance. Sweet moments between people rarely need articulation. When things between us are askew, each wants the other to put into words what the problem is. I can't think of more delicate junctures: to say enough of the truth so that you won't be lying, and less of it so that you won't be killing. At such times, I've never been more aware of the inadequacy of language, the limits of my courage. There are things we must be told, and upon their disclosure we take them in. With luck and experience, they find historical companions, buffers against the hurt. And there are simply things which never should be said. We ask to hear them, too.

Because one is always both a private and a public person, the politics of silence is far reaching. We know that silence in certain situations can be immoral. Czeslaw Milosz and Carolyn Forché, to cite two notable contemporary examples, speak about the poetry of witness. We know what they mean. But all good poetry is the poetry of witness, albeit not always to the "great" events of our time. Doubtless there are times when it is essential to make oneself heard, and we also know how many times most of us have failed others, not to mention ourselves, in this regard. The history books are full of saints, martyrs, and other sorts of radicals. In comparison to them, isn't everyone else's history a history of complacency and shame? (I'm not trying to make a case for inaction, merely to suggest that for many of us poetry comes at least as much out of attention to the unseen, the ineffable, as to the conspicuous.)

Silence, philosophically, is a subject larger than these ruminations can be equal to. To "hold one's tongue" can be either moral or immoral or neither, depending on the context. As far as silence goes, I have committed all of its errors.

In 1967 my wife and I quit our good-paying jobs and went to live in Spain. I had been storing things up; I wanted to see if I could write a novel. I was 28 years old. We had $2,200 and made it last eleven months, during which I wrote part of a poor novel, and began to write poetry. (It seemed like what I should have been writing all along.) Toperoff visited with his new wife. They liked what I was doing, and recommended graduate writing programs. I had never heard of such programs. Besides, my undergraduate grades weren't good enough, I protested. Really, I was thinking, Don't you have to *speak* in graduate school, perhaps teach? They said my poetry would get me in. They even sent away for applications for me.

In graduate school at Syracuse I did teach, wore black shirts to class so the students wouldn't see the sweat stains around my armpits, and rediscovered that freshmen were even more insecure than I. It was a fine surprise that I had things to say to them. It took me considerably longer to speak in my graduate classes, but one day in Philip Booth's poetry workshop I found myself making more sense than the brilliant but convoluted student who usually held forth, heard myself being reasonably cogent, and offered my two cents worth from then on. I was thirty.

It is interesting that in central Pennsylvania where my wife grew up, the country people use the word "backward" as a synonym for shy. It is not an insult. If I had grown up there, I would have been called backward. The citizens would have been knowingly and unknowingly correct. I was shy *and* I didn't know very much. Still whenever I feel backward, I do not speak.

On the other hand, as my involvement in the family secret suggests, my other silences originate from knowledge, from knowing more than I dare say.

Of the two kinds of silence, the one that results from ignorance is the most correctable. The other is transformable, and maybe goes to the hidden heart, if not art, of poetry. If anything has, poetry has given me the confidence to speak. First on the page, and then – as if control of words in one venue gives a useful illusion of control in another – out loud, in the public of the classroom where I can manage to conceal the subterranean streams of my ignorance. Nevertheless, I prefer a dark booth in the corner of a dark bar, one chosen person across from me.

"Silence has a rough, crazy weather," one child wrote when I visited The Katzenbach School for the Deaf. I could only imagine what it must be like in the weather of perpetual silence. But rough and crazy I understood, and the irony was not lost on me that I was in a position to teach the silent who had many things to say.

The education of my silence is ongoing, and I hope subject to revision. I've used silence cruelly as a form of disapproval or punishment, and I've often babbled to avoid it in awkward situations, and I'd like to think that there've been moments when I've used it nobly. To be able to use the word "use" in relation to my silence is both an achievement and an indictment. Once, my silence possessed me. Now that I possess it, I'd like to learn to better let it go, to let it find its necessary speech.

Along the way there's been the realization that silence can be a storehouse, a kind of place to keep the things of the world until they can become manageably ours. If we are not defeated by our shyness, our debilitating quietness, we may discover that we can cultivate it and now and again make it serve us. "Well-timed silence has more eloquence than speech," one Martin Tupper said. But La Rochefoucauld wrote, "Silence is the best tactic for him who distrusts himself." I have distrusted myself for more years than I've trusted myself. Silence was my tactic, my bane. Occasionally it still is. Whatever quality presently exists in my silence has arisen partly out of fear, partly out of a need to fill up that storehouse which I knew didn't belong to me yet. Often it is locked. I keep on finding and misplacing the key.

※

Artifice and Sincerity

There is no deeper dissembler than the sincerest man.

RALPH WALDO EMERSON

In the realm of feelings, the real and what is imaginary, assumed, pretended are hardly distinguishable.

HENRI PEYRE

I HAVE DISTRUSTED "SINCERE" PEOPLE FOR AS LONG AS I'VE ENCOUNtered them, people who begin sentences with "In all candor..." and conclude them without a deep enough sense of it. Yes, they mean what they say, but they usually haven't thought very hard about what they mean. In poetry, likewise, I've distrusted the unadulterated heartfelt utterance. And I've been in love with artifice for as long as I've made things up, which seems my entire life, yet I've been wary of the artificial, which through usage has come to be synonymous with contrived. In fact, "artificial" simply means "manmade." It's the opposite of "natural." But the artificial, as I would use the word(s) when speaking about poetry, occurs when one's artifice isn't good enough. When something isn't working for us we often say, "Oh, it's so contrived." When something works, we say "beautiful" or "complete," even "sincere."

Both Lionel Trilling and Henry Peyre have written important modern works on sincerity. Both trace the history of its usage and its relation to literature. Peyre, in particular, is interested in its relationship to artifice. One thrust of this essay will be to give emphasis to artifice's importance to sincerity. Rightly understood, they should be companions. Another will be to suggest that one's sincerity can be something found; it need not precede the poem. It is a process that Frost describes in his essay "Education by Poetry:" "... believing the thing into existence, saying as you go more than you even hoped you were going to be able to say, and coming with surprise to an end that you foreknew only with some sort of emotion." And still another thrust will be to suggest that sincerity, in some poems and maybe the best poems, might be beside the point.

Sincerity is derived from the Latin *sincerus* – clean or sound, or pure. Artifice from the Latin *artificium* – art linked with "to make." Artifice, thought of positively, suggests skill and ingenuity. But not far behind those words in most dictionaries is "a clever device, trick." Sincerity, on the other hand, is rather consistently defined as "free from pretense, genuine, real." Sincerity has the best press, though I'm not sure it's always desirable to be free from pretense. Certainly it isn't in art, but I'd like to think that sometimes in one's life, too, pretense can be a virtue, the appropriate mask, say, for the appropriate situation.

Sincerity has been extolled in some centuries, devalued in others. It is the more problematical word of the two because our sense of what "the self" is has changed so much. Once, as Peyre points out, we could believe in "an honest soul." Once, we didn't know very much about the unconscious, or about moral relativism, or about sociobiology. Once, we thought utterance was simple.

As I've said, I distrust sincere people. I also distrust, save for a few surpassing exceptions, sincere poem-makers, those persons terribly in earnest. Sincerity implies a lack of play and inventiveness. Sincere, terribly earnest poets don't entertain enough opposites, don't frolic enough with possibilities. They say, Let me tell you how I feel, or Let me tell you how it is; they rarely discover more than they knew. In fact, usually they're smug about what they know. They need an artificer for a buddy. They need to be distracted from themselves, to get beyond themselves. Schiller said, "Man only plays when he is in the fullest sense a human being, and he is only a human being when he plays." If that is true, then one complains about overly earnest people because they are half-people. Similarly, the arch artificer, who can be accused of only employing cleverness and tricks just to be clever and tricky, is a half-person. At their best, poets extend and violate all isms and theories, not because they don't care about isms and theories, but because in the writing of the poem they develop a new fidelity, which is to the language and spirit of the poem itself. This fidelity is equivalent to a spouse playing around for sake of the marriage; a dangerous enterprise. But what is dangerous in marriage is almost always desirable in poetry. One difference between a marriage and a poem is that a poem is place for various kinds of permissions; it welcomes anything that cooperates or is in tension with something else. The more poets are able to give a home to what is contradictory, ambiguous, and unruly, the more I would trust their sincerity, if by sincerity we also mean fidelity to the complexities of experience.

Andre Gide said, "One cannot both be sincere and seem so." I take this to mean two things: Sincerity is something other than what one "honestly" asserts, and it is arrived at with the help of a mask. Trilling uses Polonius' "To thine own self be true" as an example of a certain kind of sincerity, which presumed that one could know oneself well enough to be so true. We modern Poloniuses might say, "To thine own version of oneself be true." Our task would be no less difficult; the fictive has its demands and imperatives too, the most demanding of which is coherence and order, or the illusion of such. Sincerity, in part, may be the embodiment of that illusion through style and form. Conversly, we sense insincerity in a person when the mask slips. The "honest souls" who wear no masks are not insincere. They suffer from unadulterated sincerity. Their problem is dullness, a crime that deserves maximum punishment if they happen to be poets.

What poets haven't completed a draft of a deeply felt poem which felt insincere because the rhythm was off, or one word, even *one* word, was imprecise? What poets haven't finished poems to which they've introduced details that they could imaginatively but not experientially embrace, which felt sincere and *were* sincere because they had found convincing language and rhythms? They had made the details theirs. I've told stories about deeds I've done which I had not done, things which other people did, which I suppose I envied. Every self-respecting storyteller, I'm sure, as has done the same. Can we say that sincerity is what we can *make* ours? That would make successful con artists sincere. A larger question has to be asked: What is the illusion in service of? The moralist in me wants to say no, con artists aren't sincere because their goal is description, harm. But they may be brilliantly serving their own sense of self and what to them is important, with commitment and intention. To discuss poets and con artists in the same paragraph is a kind of insult, like linking diamonds with cleverly cut glass, but I do so to further illustrate that sincerity is a problematical word. For example, the makers of cleverly cut glass are trying to imitate the appearance of a diamond. They are sincerely trying to falsify. Here Peyre is helpful. He says that sincerity should not be used as a criterion of value.

I want to feel in a poem at least the ingenuity and thoughtfulness that successful con artists would bring to their tasks. I want to feel a deep sincerity of purpose, the artifice almost invisible. But of course I want the poem to be in service of some emotional and/or intellectual veracity, either by intent or some sweet accident of process.

Most poets don't have terribly noble motives. My favorite motive for writing arrived in a letter from a woman, Terry Blackhawk, who had been in a summer workshop of mine. She wrote, "The world, finally, tries to rob us in lots of ways. I like poems to do a bit of taking back for us." But most poets simply follow their obsessions; at best, they wish to use all of their resources to make something true and complete. Though they may be involved with self as much as any con artist, the best poets are saved from solipsism because of their inevitable allegiance to the poem itself; to the thing outside of them, and without regard for what rewards or spoils it might bring. In the pursuit of making something true and complete, poets, often in spite of themselves, confer value. Con artists, of course, don't. No value accrues to anyone but themselves. Sincerity aside, con artists give artifice a bad name.

Are there instances in which sincerity is beside the point? I can hear my friend the cultural anthropologist say, "What about the trickster?" The trickster, a distant cousin of the con artist, disturbs the tribe he lives in by acting contrary to its mores. He plays and incites; he causes people to react and change. He is irrepressible. One manifestation of him is the court jester, the only one who can make fun of the king. Another is the picaresque hero, who behaves with the kind of blithe disregard for convention that makes him attractive. The trickster figure is closer to the poet than to the con artist in that he doesn't have a plan; he acts out of his own genius or perversity, or both. A Rimbaud, perhaps. Or, currently, perhaps Russell Edson. Sincerity is a word that isn't useful to apply to such people. Sincerity implies, I think, some consciousness of effects. (Edson is not purely a trickster; I do think he's finally conscious of his effects.) But the "unconscious" poets are no less valuable because the structures of sincerity can't be applied to them. The trickster may in fact be operating without concern for others. The results of his actions, however, usually benefit others. It should be noted that the trickster employs artifice as he goes about his business, though he probably wouldn't own up to it if accused.

The use of pure artifice, devoid of moral issue, is apparent in the work of that half brother of the poet, the magician. We judge a magician entirely by the success of his artifice. If the rabbit is not in the hat when it is supposed to be, the act is over, or has collapsed. We trust a magician by how well he fools us, and by how well he conceals the devices he uses. We would never say a magician is sincere. His enterprise obviates the term. On one level, poets have to be at least as good as magicians. I tell my students that the first moment a poem breaks the illusion it's creating, say something as small as a misspelled word, I start reading like the critic. The act is over. Yet most poets are different from magicians in that their actions and gestures wish to point to realities outside of the poem. Serious poets *must* be magicians, but they must in some way engage the larger world we live in. Artifice serves this end; it is not an end in itself. When it is, as, for example, in "Jabberwocky," a brilliant and magical poem, we find ourselves in the presence of performance only, a system of effects which wholly satisfies, but which has no correlatives outside of it. One reason that so many of us like that poem, besides that it's so delightful, is that in reading it we never have to think about our lives or ourselves.

But to say so is not to criticize Carroll. The poem lacks the "high seriousness" someone like Matthew Arnold wanted from poems, but Carroll wasn't aspiring, in this case, to high seriousness. Moreover, the poem occurred within a larger context. In "Jabberwocky" Carroll exhibited sincerity (a purity, if you will) of composition. When Arnold says that "high seriousness comes from absolute sincerity" he errs in the other direction. His criterion is much too singularly moral, though we know that what he wants is the feel of the genuine. Most poems need

Carroll's compositional energy and esprit to achieve high seriousness. They tend not to have it when they are too purposeful.

Arnold said, "Poetry should be a criticism of life," and I think it should be, too. I also think it should be an elucidation of life, a celebration of life, an addition to life, an emblem of the mysteries of life, etc. I embrace his notion of high seriousness, but I would amend it by saying that it needs a requisite artifice to produce the illusion of absolute sincerity. Or, as is sometimes the case, sincerity, conventionally defined, is irrelevant. Did he really mean what he said? Usually the wrong question. The issue is, was he good enough to make us believe it?

Clearly, I'm talking about a poetry that aspires to art. There is of course a poetry that doesn't, in which sincerity is a given and artifice is largely unconscious. This is the poetry found in sacred texts and in prayers, say, or chants. I feel the need to acknowledge such poetry, but I'll do little more than that in this essay. We all know what myths are: They are other people's sacred texts. We treat them as literature. The people for whom they were meant simply believe them. Secretly, I suspect, all of us who write wish for such a heterogeneous community wedded by common concerns, in which our poems, if not revered, would become at least the daily news. Topics like sincerity and artifice arise only because we are talking to strangers, and we have to find artful ways to get them to trust us.

Nevertheless, we would guess that in all cultures the stories which survived, that became sacred, were the best stories, the best prayers, told by the best conjurers and tellers. People who put the best words in the best order and gave them a music. This presumes, to some degree, artfulness, though not necessarily art.

If we look at the Twenty-third Psalm, which by my lights is great poetry, we see and feel something constructed. Even though many of the psalms feel as if they were composed by committee, this one has on it throughout the distinctive imprint of a single maker. The author of the psalm, in the most elemental sense, believed it into existence. And we sense because of the distinctiveness of the psalm's phrasing and rhythm, that its author could believe other such feelings into existence. "Yea, though I walk through the valley of the shadow of death..." is the language of someone capable of comparable language. We can imagine that its author developed allegiances to rhythm and texture, had more than his original intention to be true to. But his original intention, whether it was a celebration of God or solace for us, or some combination of the two, was large, unambivalent, and does in fact make sincerity seem like a tepid word. Maybe sincerity is one of the last words we would think to apply to poems which matter deeply to us.

In poetry which aspires to be art (that is, most poetry) we would be hard pressed to find examples of utterance without artifice. Even in elegies and love poems where one, naively, might suspect a minimum of artifice, we mostly find examples of how large feelings are harnessed by form or are otherwise shaped into units of attention. But I want to champion that quality of feeling or thinking, that largeness, or that delicacy, which makes artifice its handmaiden. Great poems, of course, are seamless; they exist as entities, and though we know artifice played a part in their making we never can be exactly sure of the interplay between subject and handling of subject. Nevertheless we do feel in them what Emerson called "a meter-making argument," something which the devices of poetry had to be in service of, and be equal to. Frost said it this way in "The Constant Symbol":

> Every single poem written regular is a symbol small or
> great of the way the will has to pitch into commitments
> deeper and deeper to a rounded conclusion and then be
> judged for whether any original intention it had has been
> strongly spent or weakly lost; … Strongly spent is synony-
> mous with kept.

An original intention strongly spent. Or a discovered intention strongly spent. We really don't want sincerity from poetry any more than we want it from a flower or a finely made watch. We want something that is so wholly itself that it can be ours. Here, we say, isn't this wonderful? Look at this. Listen to it.

The Truth: a Memoir

THIS IS WHAT HAPPENED: JANUARY IN MINNESOTA. A FRIDAY afternoon. It had been snowing for about two hours, the temperature below zero. The forecast blizzard had arrived. The college (at which I was a newly hired assistant professor) called off classes at noon, but those of us with a distance to go were advised to remain and use the college as a shelter. Food would be provided. Cots.

To get home I'd have to drive thirteen miles on a two-lane road. But it was a Friday afternoon, I told myself, and I didn't want to spend the weekend in a college cafeteria. Besides, my wife and one-year-old would be alone. Fearless, I scraped the car windows, the man who had weathered New York City most of his life and had never been mugged. The windchill was minus 60. It took half an hour to go two miles. The land was flat and open. Prairie. There was nothing to deter the wind, and the blowing snow increasingly prevented me from discriminating between road and cornfield. I could beat this. So what if it took an hour or two.

The front window iced up. I could barely see out of it. But it was a straight road, and I could drive in what seemed like a straight line, now and then opening the side window to confirm where I was. That, of course, let in the cold. I started thinking: Maybe I won't make it. Maybe I should turn around. But it was impossible to turn around, I'd get stuck. And I was almost halfway. Around this time I realized I wasn't on the road. I got out of the car. Whiteness. The kind of whiteness one could easily allegorize into evil. "Poet found frozen to death in cornfield." I could see my wife reading the headlines. Or "Professor from the East exhibits hubris on the northern plains, and pays." That from a student on the school paper who was alert when I discussed Oedipus. I got back in the car. Already my beard had frozen. Gas tank half full, or was it half empty? Two candy bars in the glove compartment, my only concession to the danger of Minnesota winters.

I would die, either in the car our outside of it. I decided to walk, don't ask me why. Actually there was a reason, though it didn't become evident right away. When I looked up I could see telephone wires. Telephone wires led to telephones, and telephones lived warmly inside houses.

Perhaps the reader now is starting to lose interest. He or she can see the outcome: I followed the telephone wires to a house and was saved. The reader concludes that I was lucky, but egregiously stupid. Perhaps a beautiful woman opened the door. No, that would be a cheap narrative touch. Desperation, really, in storyteller terms. And I want to sustain, for a while longer at least, a different sense of desperation.

The fact was that after a few minutes I could see the blur of a farmhouse in the near distance. But more significantly I was freezing and overwhelmed by the desire to sleep, to lie right down in the snow and sleep. I had to repeat to myself, "There are poems to write, love to be made. Poems to write, love to be made." My mantra. When I got to the door, I literally (remember that word) fell against it in B-movie fashion. I may have knocked, but I don't remember. An old farm couple opened the door and let me in. Gave me blankets. Soup. When I sufficiently recovered I used their warm phone to call my wife. But the snow kept accumulating and I had to spend three days with them, a disagreeable couple if truth be known, but my saviors.

I've told this story for years, and only one thing is wrong with it, if in fact it constitutes a wrong. It never happened to me. I left school that day as soon as classes were called. The snow and wind were bad, but not prohibitive. I arrived home forty-five minutes later than would have been normal, and spent the weekend happily snowed-in with my family. It was my friend Al Zolynas who got lost in a cornfield. It was he who was saved by a farm couple, lovely people with whom he became friends. He spent one night, not three days, with them. Over the years I've added little touches of verisimilitude, like wishing to sleep in the snow. After all, the story is mine now. I've claimed it for whatever dark needs. Surely it could have happened to me, and something in me wished that it had. I've always desired to enlarge the life I live, only occasionally through deed.

The fictionist of self, as I've said in a poem, wants "to own his own past, / be able to manage it / more than it managed him." But my story suggests that the fictionist might want to own even more than his own past. He might want to appropriate the kindred and/or exciting deeds of others. He might want to enlarge himself by what he can credibly embrace.

Some would simply think me a liar. They might be right, but I suspect that they'd be the kind of truth-tellers inclined at dinner parties to recount their illnesses.

Obviously, lie or fiction (or both), this story is harmless enough. Yet you might despair, as my wife sometimes does, if you lived with me. Can I believe anything he says? She often wonders. Just as I often wonder (because she will not make things up) if it's possible for her to tell more than literal truths. Still, I understand why she despairs. It's one of the many drawbacks of being intimate with a writer. I love her for the many times she's not corrected me in public. It may be the most that I can ask.

She draws the line when it comes to the story of how we met. This of course is understandable, but my version (I must say) has a little more drama to it and a certain symmetry, and a faithfulness to those facts that serve to charm. Hers is simply accurate. Isn't the major responsibility of the storyteller, or of anyone who chooses to tell a story to another, to be interesting? She would say: Not always.

In my poem "The Parable of the Fictionist" I say that he "sometimes longed for what he'd dare not alter / or couldn't, / something immutable or so lovely / he might be changed / by it, / nameless but with a name / he fears waits until you're worthy, / then chooses you." I suspect that the great events of our lives do choose us as often as we choose them. Though they may and should be sacrosanct, very few of them are immutable. In essence, they are emotionally incomplete without the stories that shape and subjectify them. Great events, especially, have a parafactual life. When we start talking about them we are already changing them.

I've repeated the story of my blind date with Liza Minnelli many times. Even my wife knows it to be true, because it was one of the things

I told her during our courtship. I was seventeen or eighteen when it oc-
curred. At the time my only distinction was that I was a good basketball
player, somewhat famous at the local schoolyard in Queens. One Sat-
urday afternoon, two guys from that schoolyard that I knew slightly and
only by first names, Ike and Ron, knocked on my front door. Would I
want to go out on a date that night with Judy Garland's daughter? No
one in 1957 would have known the name Liza Minnelli. It seemed their
friend had gotten sick, couldn't go. They were desperate and thought of
me. I said okay. I told my parents (I was living at home) that I was going
out that night with Judy Garland's daughter, which to my surprise
alarmed them. They thought I was lying, covering up some other in-
tention, probably criminal or dangerous. That's the problem, some-
times, with the truth.

We took the subway to Manhattan, Ike and Ron and Ron's girlfriend.
Ike's girlfriend was the one who lived in Manhattan and knew Liza.
Both girls lived on Sutton Place, a high-rent district, another world to me.

Liza answered the door right away, so I never got to meet Judy Gar-
land or Vincente Minnelli. She was tall, maybe fifteen or sixteen, funny-
looking (I thought), and not overly enthused with me. We instantly had
nothing to say to each other, and this continued through most of the
evening, which consisted of a movie on the East Side, then ice cream at
a place called Addie Vallins. My treat. There were no other choices back
then, even though I worked as a checkout boy in Food Fair and was the
son of Charles and Ellen Dunn, vacuum cleaner salesman and house-
wife respectively.

The people to whom I've told this story, duly impressed, usually ask,
"Come on, tell us the real story. What was she really like? Did you kiss
her?" I say she was ordinary and no, nothing happened. I walked her
home, said goodbye, and experienced that relief we feel when we're
alone finally after a lousy date. I never saw her again. When I apparently
downplay the enormity of the event, I've learned that people are more
impressed, certainly more convinced that it happened. I assure them it
was an unimportant episode in my life, though of course I'm telling it,
giving it importance.

And now, to my darling wife, and those many others to whom I've
related this story, I confess it never happened. Ike and Ron (I can't

remember their real names) did knock on my door, did ask me to go out on a blind date that night with Judy Garland's daughter. I said no. I had a date that night with Barbara Beyer, who actually knew and liked me. *She* was enormously impressed that I could have gone out with Judy Garland's daughter, and no doubt I've been trying to instill in my listeners (by telling the Liza story) that near awe which registered on Barbara Beyer's face when I told her about my opportunity. Barbara was sweeter to me that night than ever, more generous with her gifts. I may have been trying to recapture such spoils with every future telling.

I wonder now if I'll ever be able to tell that story again. Telling it here may cancel it forever. But maybe I have two stories now, the false one and the coming-clean one. I think I can envisage an audience for each.

What I'm about to tell now occurred in Minnesota, as did the first story. I lived in southern Minnesota for three years, a city boy from the East, and love it and its people. I especially loved the uncynical intelligence of my best students, and how open they were to learning. I hadn't been back in five years, and was very much looking forward to giving a poetry reading and seeing old friends. The college sent a young woman, an aspiring writer, in a state car to pick me up at the airport in Minneapolis.

But before I say what happened (a word you must be suspicious of by now) I should mention that I had just purchased new, expensive shoes. This was no small thing. My wife had been after me for quite a while to own shoes that were other than desert boots or sneakers. After all, I was almost respectable now.

The student in the state car was lovely, bright, interesting — a little older than the regular undergraduate. It was a two-and-a-half-hour drive to my destination, and we talked famously. Too famously, as it turned out. She hadn't been checking the gas gauge. About forty-five minutes from my friend Howard Mohr's house (where I was to have dinner before the reading) the car started to sputter. But she was a farm girl and this was farm country. Just before the car lost all power she pulled brilliantly into a farmhouse. A young farmer came out to ask what the problem was. It should be mentioned that it was April. Thawing time. She got out of the car to talk to him, to ask if he had any gas. I stayed put. He was out of gas, but his father owned a farm about ten miles away and he'd get us some. That's how I remembered Minnesota people: generous, especially when you were in trouble. He got in his pickup and left.

I noted that Carol, the young woman, had noted that I didn't get out of the car. It would have been common decency to do so, especially in Minnesota, where men were expected to deal with men. But the mud, you see, was a foot deep, and I had on my new shoes.

The farmer returned with the gas, and she got out of the car again to pay and talk to him while he poured it from a five-gallon can. I stayed put. We thanked him and said good-bye. But as we started out the car got stuck in the mud. The farmer got behind the car to push. I knew I should help, but hesitated, and finally it was too late. He was a mud ball by the time he shook us loose.

Carol didn't speak to me the rest of the way. I was mortified by my behavior, knew what it meant. But my shoes still looked fine, even though they felt a little conspicuous now, a little heavier, like Pinocchio's nose.

The few times I've told this story everyone has laughed and affectionately scolded me. They liked that I could tell such an appalling story on myself. It seems to be a good story as stories go. But what I've left out is this. That night after the reading Carol asked me how someone who could write such sensitive poems could have been so insensitive back at the farm. I told her I didn't know. And then she kissed me straightaway on the lips. I watched her the entire night at the party. I knew that later we would find each other, and that she would allow me to expiate my guilt through her, and that she would offer herself as if she were the mud-and-shoe saint of Minnesota to this man from the East who needed some soul-work. I took off my shoes back in her room. I wept a little at the sight of her. She was disgusted with herself afterwards.

Why I left out this coda to my story is because I just invented it. Carol never spoke to me after the reading; she wanted nothing to do with me. The melodramatist in me had her kiss me, forgive and shame me, and take off her clothes. I'm sorry, I couldn't help myself.

However, everything that happened on the road and on the farm was true, though some might argue no more or less true than my coda. I'm not sure that it matters. What matters in this instance is that my mud-and-shoes story seemed to need an extra touch, and that Carol (who was crucial early in the story) return in a manner that would relate to the teller's (my) moral failure. What do I hold dear enough not to alter? Here is where the story of how I met my wife might be relevant.

My wife, after all, has been a character in this slippery memoir. She, too, needs to be carried forward. There is something sacred to me about how we met, which is how she made me feel, and the magic of that particular day. In my telling I try to be true to that magic, much as Monet was trying to be true to the feel and look of the light when he painted lilies. Yes, the lilies were important, but anyone could paint lilies. The light was what mattered. When I tell the story of how we met I know that the details must be at least approximate, if not sometimes exact. Yet I'm mostly after emotional veracity, as I am in every poem I write. Always there are a few touches, a few shadings, that can serve that veracity.

But for now I'll just offer the bare facts. We met during one of the biggest snowstorms in New York City history. I'm committed to this snowstorm. (If I didn't have at least some allegiance to fact, I'd make it a hurricane or power blackout.) I began this piece with a blizzard. A blizzard and a snowstorm in such close proximity is risky business, if your business is writing. In fiction, the two together would constitute a narrative error, and lack of imagination. Yet a snowstorm it was, and is.

She had taken a temporary job in the office at which I worked, and I'd been watching (read "coveting") her for about a week. By this time I knew that we traveled the same subway. We hadn't spoken prior to the day of the storm, but that very morning I had sent her (via a friendly mail boy) an anonymous message, which began "Dear No Name," containing what amounted to all I knew of flirtatious wit. The office decided to close early because of the storm. So had almost every office in the city. I followed her to the subway, where, amid thousands, I told her that it was I who had written the note.

When the train finally came, the situation was worse than at rush hour, but we managed to get on, and were instantly pressed together, front to front, more tightly than if we had been hugging. Because of the weather, the train was very slow. Very, very slow. By the time we reached our destination there was much to build on. In her purse (I didn't know this) was a one-way airline ticket to Miami to meet a man she had decided to live with. I still remember — one week later in her apartment

—when he called and she said she was sorry, she had changed her mind.

In her version the same things happen, though in slightly different sequence. And she usually delineates the circumstances of her past that led her to this historical juncture. And in a few of my versions, *many* more things happen, though just how many usually depends on how receptive the company is and the élan of the moment. For example, when we emerge from the subway station, the snow is up to our waists. We know by this time that we don't want to leave each other, that something large already has been set in motion. We have soup at a nearby diner. A few drinks at a nearby bar. We go to the movies, and hold hands like teenagers. We are both delaying and moving toward the walk to her apartment. What will happen there will be momentous, will change our lives and we almost know this. It's after midnight when we start out, nine hours since the office closed, everything is crystalline and silent, no footprints but ours on the obscured residential streets. We do not speak, afraid of what we'll say, or that we might trivialize what we feel, what we fear. We kiss at her door. In some versions I'm invited in. In some I'm not. In one version, opening a bottle of wine, I break her antique table, though that in fact happened a few days later. In another, she has a roommate who counsels her to give me up, which she considers. I walk out in a huff and go to see *Last Year at Marienbad* at the corner theater, come back in love with solitude and mystery, which alters me forever. For me to see that movie, I must rearrange the story's time sequence. This I happily do.

Oscar Wilde has, for me, the greatest wisdom on this subject:

> It is possible, of course, that I may exaggerate [about the essays of Pater]. I certainly hope that I do; for when there is no exaggeration there is no love, and where there is no love there is no understanding. It is only about the things that do not interest one, that one can give really unbiased opinion; and that no doubt is why an unbiased opinion is always so absolutely worthless.

Over the twenty-seven years of our marriage, the "facts" of our meeting have blended with other facts, or have simply been changed, though what I consider the central details remain. And though she didn't intend it, her objections to these alterations — like any good criticism — have led to improvements. For one, it seems that in early versions I made myself out too much as the hero of the story. This upset her, justifiably. For her complaint I'm grateful. She saved me from being an unconscious unreliable narrator. My latest version is better now, cleaner, and no doubt truer.

Alert Lovers, Hidden Sides, and Ice Travelers: Notes on Poetic Form & Energy

"THREE FORCES," NABOKOV WROTE, "MAKE AND MOLD A HUMAN being: heredity, environment, and the unknown agent x. Of these the second, environment, is by far the least important, while the last, agent x, is by far the most influential."

I'm not going to speculate about how people are molded, but rather how poems are, with an eye to what may be the poetic equivalent of agent x. I want to start by making some simpler observations about the formal properties of free verse, and conclude by talking about ice travelers, the kind of formalists I most like.

All poetry has formal properties, and free verse poets have to be especially sensitive to this, working as we do to create not only the shapes within the container (to paraphrase Roethke), but the shape of the container itself. That is, we must know that with the very first lines we put down we've created a series of promises and expectations in terms of diction, line, texture, rhythm, and of course content, and we must live up to these promises or satisfactorily defy or play off of them. The manner in which we keep our promises is one way in which form comes about.

There are some well-known definitions: Creeley's "Form is no more than the extension of content." Levertov's improvement, "Form is the revelation of content." And one that I've always remembered because it sounds sexual and because of its simplicity, "Form is the arousal and fulfillment of desires," which is Kenneth Burke's.

When writing think like a lover, is how I choose to understand
Burke. It's in one's interest to fulfill desires once aroused. The bad lover
like the bad poet, perhaps because of a preoccupation with self, is es-
sentially inattentive, doesn't listen, doesn't anticipate. Or, just as bad,
proceeds by rote, first this thing and then the next, and therefore leaves
no opportunity for discovery, or departure. Form to me implies an alert-
ness to the demands of your material and an orchestration of effects. It
is some happy combination of the poet's intent and the poem's *esprit*
and the necessary compromises between the two. We can't be too will-
ful, but we must have things in mind. We don't want to be the wimps of
our own poems, but we'd be happy to be led into some lovely places.
And we'd like to have some control after we lose control, at least enough
to throw light on what has just happened, perhaps even to articulate
what it has meant to us. And of course there are moments when we'd be
better off being appreciatively silent.

What I've just said suggests a significant if not a full consciousness of
the elements we put in our poems, and of course there are poems in
which such a consciousness is possible. Most poets can control at least
one level of meaning, sometimes two levels, and can sustain a poem's
surface effects. Certainly this is true post-composition, in the revision
process. But often poems have hidden formal properties that are not
so easily identified. Vasko Popa's "Prudent Triangle" (translated by
Charles Simic) might be a paradigm for what I have in mind.

PRUDENT TRIANGLE

Once upon a time there was a triangle
It had three sides
The fourth it kept hidden
In its burning center

By day it climbed its three peaks
And admired its center
At night it rested
In one of its three angles

Each dawn it watched its three sides
Turn into three fiery wheels
And vanish in the blue of never return

It took its fourth side
Embraced and broke it three times
To hide it again in its old place

And again it had only three sides
And again it climbed each day
To its three peaks
And admired its center
While at night it rested
In one of its angles

The triangle with a fourth side is a wonderful figure for the hidden propulsive element in a poem. Perhaps the triangle is prudent because, although it has a fourth side, an agent x, a side that is very active all day long, "at night it rested / in one of its angles." The triangle, therefore, knows when not to be active, when it's better off "admiring its burning center." In poetic terms, at some point it has distance, aesthetic distance, which of course is analogous to Popa's participation in his own poem.

The fourth side is the agent of heat. It's a propulsive force, altering our conventional understanding of the triangle. It causes the triangle's three sides to "turn into three fiery wheels / and vanish in the blue of never return." (The triangle just "watches" this happen, implying that what it has set in motion has imperatives of its own). Then the triangle takes its fourth side and breaks it "three times / to hide it again in its old place." (Here the triangle is active and full of intention.) I take this as a metaphor for the poem's energy, the energy that is a combination of the poet's intentionality and the poem's vibrant, increasingly insistent demands. The hidden side both informs the poem and is an element in the poem. If the fourth side is the agent x, then the activity of the triangle is akin to how poets inhabit their poems. The triangle is the orchestrator of its mysteries, sometimes admiring its elements from afar, sometimes watching as its parts seem to act by themselves, sometimes very close and involved, embracing and breaking. It would be wrong to push Popa's little parable too far, but at the very least it has usefully pointed me to this conclusion: a discussion about a poem's form is often incomplete unless it identifies a poem's central concerns, its main propulsive forces.

It may seem odd to move from "burning centers" to ice travelers, but

I hope only for a short while. I borrow my metaphor of ice traveling from William Meredith's fine love poem, "Crossing Over." In that poem the speaker and his lover are out on a river of steadily melting ice, and Meredith uses this situation to reflect upon the precariousness of love. "I contemplate this unfavorable aspect of things," the speaker says mid-poem, and after ruminating about what's solid and what isn't, he concludes the poem with these lines:

> Here all we have is love, a great undulating
> raft, melting steadily. We go out on it
>
> anyhow. I love you. I love this fool's walk.
> The thing we have to learn is how to walk light.

We go out on it anyhow. That's what ice travelers and lovers and poets do in the face of difficulty and even danger. Let's say, for the sake of making distinctions of value, there are poets who are ice travelers and poets who are ice skaters, even some that are sedentary ice fishers. Though the latter two may come up with pleasing results, the ice traveler is always willing and able to go a little farther, perhaps even deeper. When confronted with, say, the perverse, the chaotic, the unknown, the ice traveler poet is in his or her real territory, and seeks to find a structure in which such things can live. Often, however, poets avoid or don't arrive at their real subjects. This is one kind of skater's poem, or maybe an early draft of an ice travelers poem. That is, it can be remedied if the poet is able to break back into the poem and locate its true concerns. The other kind of skater's poem is more annoying, the poem of only surface-effects, the poet-skater confident that the ice will keep him safe while he does a few dazzling figure-eights, which are small pleasures for everyone. These are the poems that usually don't invite us to return to them. Having said that, I should say that I think the poem's hidden subject *can* be on the surface. It can exist in juxtapositions and arrangements, or perhaps be the discoverable radiance of all the words together. But, in general, beware the skater. Welcome the ice traveler, trying to get to the other side without taking the easy way, slipping now and then, always interested in what it means to stay alive.

The compositional problems of ice travelers have something to do with the pressure their movements exert. Each word they add, each new claim they make, results in the necessity of new accommodations. To successfully get out of the poem becomes that much more problematical. Don't we often feel *stranded* in a poem? Somehow the new detail that's been added, for the moment at least, won't permit us to carry the poem forward. Here's the ice traveler's paradox. This problem is eliminated when he's compositionally *hot*, when the poem is "riding on its own melting." For ice travelers this translates into annihilation. And maybe annihilation of the self, or at least self-consciousness, is the condition to which every good poem aspires. That is the death that revivifies. It is desirable to be compositionally *hot*, one thing flowing immediately into another, and equally desirable that the efforts and struggles involved in making the poem disappear by the time the poem is finished. A poem "riding on its own melting" suggests both diminishment and accretion, and may take us back to the triangle that breaks up and hides its fourth side. The fourth side hasn't gone away; it's just not visible. One formal achievement may reside in drawing no attention to form.

There are as many kinds of ice travelers as there are varieties of good poets, but the quintessential ice travelers risk falling in because they trust what they're connected to, long ropes made of skill and insight which they believe will rescue them from danger. What I wish to say is that the farther we go in a poem or on the ice the fewer and fewer choices we have, and we would want it no other way. We are limited by the choices of diction and rhythm that we've already employed, and by the poem's contextual logic. Only if we've been compositionally sloppy do we have manifold choices at the end of a poem. Prufrock cannot suddenly become Don Juan. A meditative poem should not suddenly become rhapsodic, unless a pattern is about to form. Poems must advance themselves and deepen as they proceed, and the ideal ice travelers are both pressing down and "walking light" (which is William Meredith's advice for ice-walking and navigating the difficulties of love). They're pressing down with their entire weight (that is, everything they can bring to bear on the subject). And they're walking light, employing the appropriate skill for the task. You might want to jump up and down and shout in ecstasy at the top of an emotional mountain (I like some of those poets, too). You might be a leaping poet on flat ground, say in Minnesota. But on thin ice you need a different approach. Generally speaking, good poets always, by the end of their poems, intuitively or otherwise, know where they are.

Risk is an overrated word when it comes to poetry writing and successful ice traveling. In Barry Lopez' wonderful book *Arctic Dreams* he says this about going out on a dangerous expedition in the Arctic:

> My companions, all scientists, were serious about this
> (leaving a note in their cabin about the time they
> left, the expected time of return as well as their
> compass bearing — parenthesis mine), but not solemn or
> tedious. They forestalled trouble by preparing for it,
> and were guided, not deterred, by the danger inherent
> in their work. It is a pleasure to travel with such
> people. As in other walks of life, the person who
> feels compelled to dramatize the risks or is either
> smugly complacent or eager to demonstrate his survival
> skills is someone you hope not to meet.

Experienced ice travelers tend to put themselves in the middle of a big lake; let's call it Lake Eros. They want to walk light with their entire beings, and to do so they need to know as much as they can about the history of ice in, say, February, in this particular climate, and what other ice travelers have accomplished before them, and be utterly modern too; that is, they need to know the tradition *and* what's in the air now, and be alert to the unforeseen, which is the nature of the enterprise. The risk is placing themselves out there knowing that their movements generate pressure, and therefore problems, and the more they surprise themselves the more difficult it will be to get to shore. But they will have spent years preparing themselves for such problems.

Skaters work only the safe part of the lake. And ice fishers, those earnest poets, well, it is obvious, often too obvious, what ice fishers are doing. In some climates, of course, they build a little shack on the ice, and thus conspicuously formalize the act of fishing. When they catch a fish, we say yes, we knew they would, and usually we've seen the fish before. Ice travelers are less purposeful. They have their own way of fishing, and they don't stop their traveling to fish. They like to be out on the ice and they like to keep moving. Their fishing is more magical. When they pass over the ice just right, spectacular fish break through the ice and offer themselves. These fish are recognizably fish, but they have no names. The job of ice travelers is to name them. And then they toss them back, not out of pity or compassion, but because the fish they name always are for others to find, and to do with as they please. Each fish named by an ice traveler is its own statement of form. It has been caught on Lake Eros, no one knows how.

So every ice traveler knows that, sometimes, form is as much something found as it is something willed or honed. For ice travelers there always is ice. They are nothing if not imaginative. They are the ones who keep moving toward the other side, though happy to take detours. Their goal is to disappear while leaving evidence of their journey. It's to make a livable environment for what's hidden, rearrange what's already known.

Most of us are pure ice travelers only a few times in our lives. More often we are some composite of ice traveler and alert lover. We live in some angle of our poem, sometimes in its center (if not burning center), sometimes coolly watching, shaping. Out of habit and necessity we come to the ice of the white page. We place ourselves where something can happen, and press down, hoping we can find something central and edgy to move us along. Form takes its cue from what we find ourselves saying. And then it attempts to give that saying the feel and look of permanence.

Philip Booth's poem "Saying It," I think, says and exemplifies much of what I've been discussing.

SAYING IT

Saying it. Trying
to say it. Not
to answer to

logic, but leaving
our very lives open
to how we have

to hear ourselves
say what we mean.
Not merely to

know, all told,
our far neighbors;
or here, beside

us now, the stranger
we sleep next to.
Not to get it said

and be done, but to
say the feeling, its
present shape, to

let words lend it
dimension: to name
the pain to confirm

how it may be borne:
through what in
ourselves we dream

to give voice to,
to find some word for
how we bear our lives.

Daily, as we are daily
wed, we say the world
is a wedding for which,

as we are constantly
finding, the ceremony
has not yet been found.

What wine? What bread?
What language sung?
We wake, at night, to

imagine, and again wake
at dawn to begin: to let
the intervals speak

for themselves, to
listen to how they
feel, to give pause

to what we're about:
to relate ourselves,
over and over; in

time beyond time
to speak some measure
of how we hear the music:

today if ever to
say the joy of trying
to say the joy.

Booth is wholly alert to the overt formal promises he has made early and throughout his poem, and is sufficiently aware of the forces that are tacit and informative. The poem's urgency comes in part from the tension introduced in the first stanza, between "saying it" and "*Trying* to say it." We sense both the difficulty of saying it, and the necessity to do so. One of the poem's formal achievements is how well Booth's rhythms and syntax and even his punctuation score and underscore the difficulty and necessity of his enterprise. Ostensibly, the poem is "about" writing poetry, but as the language of the poem indicates it is equally and appropriately a poem about "how we bear our lives." One of the poem's not-so-hidden propulsive elements is the tacit assertion that the poem must be evidence of this struggle to bear our lives, and must paradoxically be the ceremony for the ceremony that "has not yet been found." In other words, the propulsive elements are both philosophical and aesthetic; they constantly inform the poem's choices. The poem has the feel of ice-traveling throughout, its mostly enjambed triplets structural evidence of containment and flow, claim after claim a kind of pressing down, the poet always in danger, if he were to slip, of becoming too abstract or didactic.

The poem makes several promises in its first six stanzas, the most conspicuous of which is that it is going to be built on a series of repetitions, as well as on a series of statements that will be refined and extended. We are overhearing, in Stevens' language, "The poem of the mind / in the act of finding what will suffice." The word that is going to drive the poem is "to." This and the other recurrences constitute the poem's most obvious formal properties, along with Booth's commitment to a predominantly two-stress line with largely iambic underpinnings. In addition to many trochaic substitutions, Booth manages his lines so as to break-up or delay an iambic movement, as in "to find some word *for* / how we bear our lives." He won't let the poem flow too regularly, which would work against its dramatic tensions. It's a system of language that keeps its promises while advancing its claims and, as it muses wisely about the difficulty of "saying it," it also manages onomatopoeically "to speak some measure / of how we hear the music." Each additional "to" presses down a little harder. The poem is going to thump home, clause after imperative clause, with just one lovely interrogative release from form: "What wine? What bread? / What language sung?" This is an example of the ice traveler knowing that the straight, linear way home may be fast, but not terribly interesting.

In an interview, Booth said about this poem that "I think I'm not talking *about* saying it. I would like to think that in some way I'm the consciousness of the poem's *being the act* of saying it." It is interesting to note that this is how Booth feels he inhabits his own poem. It's similar, I would argue, to Popa's informing consciousness in "Prudent Triangle." The triangle apparently makes its own moves, but in that little geometric universe Popa is the god who's created the terms and set them in motion. "Once upon a time," Popa says, and we're ready for the magic of fiction. Booth's statement reflects how his creation seems both his and a magical thing of its own.

If Booth's poem has a truly hidden element, an agent x, it is the joy of trying to say what is difficult to say. Arguably it exists all along in the poem's center, intimately related to difficulty and necessity. The poem concludes "…today if ever to / say the joy of trying / to say the joy." Yet Booth has chosen to title his poem "Saying It", not "Trying To Say It." By poem's end, something clearly *has* been said, though mid-poem Booth suggests that such saying is never finished: "Not to get it said / and be done, but to / say the feeling, its / present shape…", and we trust that Booth once again will be out on the ice, trying to say the shape of another feeling, perhaps even the same one in a different time "after time." Such is the life of an ice traveler. "Saying," of course, is never finished. Yet if form does give permanence to language then this poem is complete, its promises kept, its hard-earned effects fixed in time and space.

⚜

The Poet as Teacher:
Vices and Virtues

An obvious given: In this country a poet must have another job. A few poets, very few, can eke out a living from doing readings, but certainly no poet's royalties are sufficient to live on. I've long ago accepted this as the way things are. I teach. I get paid for talking about what I like to talk about, and I wish it were that simple. When I was asked by a colleague to write something about how, if at all, the teaching of poetry writing has affected my own writing, my first thought was "Maybe it has a little, but not importantly." It was my second thought too, but increasingly the question seemed to deserve a more elaborate answer.

One of the things I hear myself saying over and again to my poetry-writing students is "Your poem effectively begins at the first moment you've surprised or startled yourself. Throw away everything that preceded that moment, and begin with that moment." I go on to say that we mostly begin our poems with our ordinary, workaday minds, those minds burdened by the conventional, and if we're lucky we start to say something we didn't know we knew, and/or find phrasing that couldn't have been available to us at the outset of the poem. If we do, then we're on our way. Having said that, it's chastening to note that Frost said that anyone can get into a poem, it takes a poet to get out of one.

To the extent that the ability to isolate problem areas in other people's poems draws the teaching poet's attention to the same problems in his or her own poems, I suppose that the teaching of poetry writing for all these years has contributed in some way to my own work. But the question of whether the teaching of writing affects one's own work raises other issues; among them, competence versus excellence, and the nature of poetry itself. Personally, I can't see how it hurts, unless the regular encounter with bad poetry can be argued to be harmful, or, as I'll elaborate on later, one's teaching starts to take precedence over one's writing. On the other hand, if we wish to write truly memorable poems, which I do and most poets do, then I can't see how the teaching of poetry writing helps very much. George Seferis wrote, "To say what you want to say, you must create another language and nourish it for years with what you have loved, with what you have lost, with what you will never find again." In light of such a remark, teaching poetry seems separate indeed from the real stuff that goes into the making of a poem.

I suspect that if I aspired to be a competent poet, then the teaching of writing would help me to be just that. That is, a master of various kinds of decorum, a manager of certain pleasures, alert to the ungenuine, the downright false. But competence, the ability to fashion what looks like a poem and even to please, is the bugaboo of the creative writing teacher qua poet, and the enterprise of creative writing itself. The danger is that we can become satisfied with making things turn out satisfactorily. The well-made poem, lacking the Seferis ingredients, is increasingly in my own work what I try to avoid, though I'm sure I fail more than succeed.

In my poetry-writing workshops on the undergraduate level, I'm happy at first with competence. On the graduate level I try not to be. Over the years it's been important for me to think about why I'm in this profession at all. After all, so few of my students have turned out to be poets. If I'm not making writers, what am I doing?

First, some assumptions about language and the importance of precision. Most of the language we encounter daily is imprecise if not consciously designed to deceive. We constantly are confronted with versions of the world that don't correspond to our sense of it. On one of its levels, a poetry workshop infuses and restores a respect for precision, for finding the right words, therefore moving the writer closer to what can credibly be said about something. This is one reason why teaching still pleases me; over, say, a semester, to witness a student move in the direction of the true(r). I treat even the most marginal student's poem as a poem wishing to be a poem. I hold it to high standards, as if it might be a poem. But secretly what I know I'm doing is instructing the student about the tendency toward self-indulgence (the main problem of beginning writers), the problems of sloppy feeling and thinking, and something about what the inauthentic sounds like. It's moral instruction in the guise of crafting and editing. When teaching graduate students, all of whom are there because they wish to be poets, I'm doing the same thing, though I'm less tolerant of the merely competent poem, and seek and hold out for those distinguishing characteristics that might separate them from the horde. But in fact the major thrust of my teaching has to do with accuracy and truthfulness, which implies surprising oneself and having enough savvy to know what might surprise others. Even when a student fails to write a startling poem, there are often moments in the poem to praise — movements toward the genuine. If I remember that this is mostly what I'm doing as a teacher, helping them to move toward and identify the genuine, then I'm less disappointed when the marginal students, quite properly, decide to become social workers instead. And of course, too, the entire process makes all of them better readers. Most of my academic colleagues will attest that the creative writing students are among their most alert readers, sensitive to the ways poems and stories move and turn.

As everyone knows, you can't teach someone to be a poet. At best, you offer cautionary advice as it applies to specific, practical problems, perhaps citing a great poet's successful handling of the same problem. You praise the student's true achievements. You assign and discuss great and good poems and urge students to find their own models of excellence. Maybe you tell them some of the compelling statements writers have made about being writers, which go beyond just wanting to be wordsmiths. Gunter Kunert's: "That's why I write; to bear the world as it crumbles." Or Rilke's: "The ultimate intuitions and insights will only approach one who lives in his work and remains there, and whoever considers them from afar gains no power over them." Yet when I try to recall what I've said in workshops, I mostly remember not the high-minded things I've said but the many *be carefuls* that I've offered. Be careful of the first line that's longer or shorter than the line you've been working with; it may signal that you've fallen out of rhythm. Be careful of the first moment that you double back and return to a previous effect; it may mean that you've ceased to advance the poem, or have nothing more to say. Be careful of an ending that seems only satisfactory; there's a better one sleeping in your material if you hold out for it. Be careful that this poem truly matters to you; otherwise think of it as practice and put it aside. Be careful not to be too careful in first drafts; let the poem go, let it always find its next moment, hope that it gets away from you. These are things I've said to students for years, and now and then I listen to my own precepts. A good teacher can hasten a potential poet's development, not much more. As far as his own work goes, good teaching might help to make him a better reviser, a better editor, not much more.

A well-known poet once said that when he taught a very good class it often set his writing back a week or so. He was referring to the tremendous satisfaction that comes from teaching well. Writers, I think, know this better than non-writers because there's a common principle involved. When you teach well you start to say things you didn't know you were going to say, perhaps things you had forgotten you knew. That kind of discovery is exactly what happens in a good poem or story. After teaching well, the poet feels less urgency to go home and write. We need enormous energy both to teach and write well.

Sometimes the poet-teacher is simply beleaguered, involved in poorly paid part-time work, and/or compelled to move from job to job, state to state, almost every year. And most junior professors find themselves with many papers to grade, classes to prepare, committees to endure. In such cases, "teaching" is not the issue. It's all the demands of getting ready to teach, plus tertiary collegial obligations. There's a debilitating encroachment on writing time.

Even in good situations, the human factors in teaching poetry writing take considerable emotional energy. It's the most intimate teaching I've ever done. Though I try to treat all poems as if they were fictions, I know I'm talking about someone's life, and/or someone's creation in which there's a large ego investment. Even the most delicate criticisms hurt. At the same time, I'm aware that few other people, give or take a few shrinks, will ever again take these would-be poets' personal revelations so seriously. There's a large responsibility in that. I want them to find their hidden subject. I want them to say things they didn't know they knew, and I want them to say those things precisely and surprisingly. Students are startled when they reveal their most haunting secrets and, instead of making judgments about them, you say perhaps, "Stained would be a better word than bloody in this line." Or perhaps, more cruelly, "You've yet to make the abortion interesting for others. You haven't yet gotten beyond the confessional impulse. It's a violation of intimacy (and poor pedagogy) to discuss the personal revelation as revelation. The best intimacy between teacher and student occurs when the student trusts that the teacher is some kind of partner in helping the poem in question to become a poem. But more often, even if there is trust, the student clings to his or her creation, is not ready to hear the things that are wrong with it. It even can be argued that the students *should* cling to their creations for as long as they can; after all, some kind of gumption is going to be needed to get through the coming years of neglect. Yet for the teacher to address such understandable if unearned pride, face to face in workshops and in conferences, can be exhausting and harrowing work.

Even though I teach in a state college and do not have a cushy teaching load, I've been lucky to have a teaching schedule that affords me my mornings free. I can't complain. Teaching, on the face of it, has been better for me than most jobs would have been. I don't subscribe to the manual labor theory, popular during the sixties. To wit, work a job in which you don't use your brain, as if that would grant you greater purity and brainpower when you sat down to write. Mostly, manual labor makes you tired and therefore represents a different encroachment on time, and purity is something few of us every achieve. In fact, purity for the writer may not be very desirable. Complicity always has seemed more seminal to me.

Much has been written of late about university life being injurious to the spirit and about the way it might limit the kinds of experience one might bring to a poem. There's some truth in such claims. But most of life is injurious to the spirit, and the "real world" is often as limiting as the university. The writer's burden is somehow to keep alive and vital amid all that's dangerous and deadening in the world, and this is difficult wherever one is. Stevens managed it in an insurance firm. Eliot (for a while) in a bank. The imagination is a friend of the spirit, and it travels awfully well; it really doesn't mind when you take it to a dull party. That may be exactly where it comes into its own.

In Roethke's poem "Dolor," on page 84 for example, we see the verve and the cohering powers of the poet's imagination as it takes on institutional life. The "Dust," from what we assume are office buildings and corporations, glazes "the pale hair, the duplicate gray standard faces" of those who work in them. Not to become one of the "duplicate gray standard faces" takes vigilance; it's a teacher's problem as much as it is an account executive's or a clerk's. And it's a writer's problem as well, not to become one of the gray, standard writers. To finally write like no one else. So few of us achieve such singularity that it would be foolish to blame the university for our failure to do so. This is why I find it difficult to say exactly what, if anything, teaching has meant to my writing. The clearest thing it's done is give me more time than if I'd had another job.

The rest is between the poet and the gods. It may come down to something as undemocratic and undiscussable as talent. Who knows? The good poet always surmounts circumstances, both the circumstances of his or her life and the initial circumstances of his or her poem. This is why mere competence is the enemy of good poetry. Every good poem is evidence of a step taken into the unknown or the vaguely known, from which one comes back with palpable approximations. Words for. Much apprenticeship and practice are needed to get to the point where such a step can be taken (Keats and Rimbaud notwithstanding). The act of getting there can't be taught, nor can it be willed.

Teaching is one kind of mastery, one way of knowing and becoming intimate with your subject. As I said earlier, I don't think it can hurt your writing as long as you remain more of a poet than a teacher. That's the difficult balance. When the scale tips toward teaching as your primary identity, when the struggles and pleasures of the classroom supersede the struggles and pleasures of the page, as can easily happen, that's when you must rightly call yourself teacher, an honorable enough title to be sure, but a capitulation to safer territory in which a text already exists and there's no permanent record of what you've said.

It's no accident that more good poetry arises out of crises and dilemmas than out of triumphs and jobs well done. We are less likely to confront self and world when we're satisfied with self and world. We're less likely to have that edge that leads to discovery. The poet always must be to some degree an outsider, must always be probing for what's hidden and unexplored, must always resist what passes for reality. Most poets I know don't have to be willful about this. It's a matter of temperament. Kafka's Hunger Artist, when asked why he became the way he was, said he just didn't like the food the rest of us eat. Kafka's parable suggests that the artist must be driven by obsessions and needs that are not necessarily located in the rational domain. They constitute the artist's strength against the manifold pulls toward the conventional and the great middle. This may be why few poets are granted tenure. On the other hand, the university poet who buys in too fully to being a good citizen of the university is in danger of losing his outsider's edge.

In my case, since I'm mostly inclined to be a good citizen, I'm occasionally saved by other limitations of my personality. It's not that I don't like the university's food, it's just that I don't possess the ability to eat it very well. For example, when I've found myself on committees, I rarely know what to say. Once, finding myself on something called the Priorities & Resources Committee, I vainly tried to think in those terms. My colleagues construed my silence as arrogance, but in fact it was incompetence. This kind of thing has happened often enough that I'm seldom asked to be on committees. When I am, I marvel at those who find the proper words for the occasion. Other times, my inclinations to be solitary, to withdraw, are immense. I suspect, for better or worse, these are perceived as the quirks of the poet.

Because I teach *creative writing,* it's important for me to remember that I'm not a *creative writer,* I'm a poet. It's important for me to remember to tell my students that I'm not interested in *creative* writing; I'm interested in poetry. There are many creative writers, and relatively few poets. I receive many interesting inventions. I receive many well-made verbal machines. Rarely do I receive that "clear expression of mixed feelings," that blend of "delight and wisdom," that piece of writing that "takes the top of my head off," which is poetry. Rather than find this too dispiriting, often I can take pleasure in small improvements and the flashes of the genuine that students are capable of. Granted, some days it doesn't seem worth it. At those times I need to remember that in the relative scheme of things, a small community of would-be poets is a rather tolerable place to hang out.

In the final analysis, how a fine poem comes along is mysterious, though when it happens it's clearly a transcendence of what one's job may be, even if that "job" is lucky enough to be a poet and nothing else. How many times does lightning strike? How many times does the poet get to traffic with the gods? Away from lightning, light years away from the gods, the teaching of poetry isn't a bad occupation. It may be argued that lightning hits the person in the field more than it hits the person in the university. Maybe. But the poet who teaches lives in the field too, inescapably, in the common field of love and loss and sorrow, not to mention revenge, ambiguity, deception, etc. And the gods, I have to believe, are perverse and ubiquitous, though no doubt more likely to visit those of us who habitually try to reach them.

Journal Notes

ONE PERCEPTION MUST IMMEDIATELY LEAD TO ANOTHER PERCEPTION, as Olson said, is another way of saying that a poem should be interesting *all* the way through.

When people praise a poem that I can't understand I always think they're lying.

The problem with most nature poetry is that it doesn't sufficiently acknowledge Nature's ugliness and perversity. It is as falsifying as most poems about happy marriages.

Poems about happy marriages need to be mysterious. A successful happy-marriage poem, like a happy marriage itself, is a triumph over the unlikely. You must write it with the inventive care with which you would write science fiction.

Every male has a stake in feminism. Obviously it is not a good situation for anybody when one sex has earned the greater right to complain. And don't happy women tend to be generous? Self-interest, if not basic decency, should convince men that a fair-minded feminism is also their liberation. All of us, finally, free enough to be scoundrels.

Poets who defy making sense and do it deliberately and often brilliantly (as Ashbery can) *are* making a kind of sense, and may be extending the range of what poetry can do, though they ensure that poetry's audience will be small and chiefly academic: i.e., composed of people inclined to equate a puzzle with that which is meaningful.

Mystifications protect power. Mysteries protect the sacred. – John Berger

Authenticity in literature does not come from a writer's personal honesty... Authenticity comes from a single faithfulness: that to the ambiguity of experience... If a writer is not driven by a desire for the most demanding verbal precision, the true ambiguity of events escapes him. – John Berger

When I've had an interesting or haunting dream, I know I'd better not try to write about it until it has begun to bore me a little.

A perfectly modulated sentence, one that discloses its information at just the right pace, is a victory over what is crude and easy and careless about the way we think and feel. A paragraph of such sentences has the sufficiency of a well-made sculpture. About its content, we're likely to say, "That's true." What we mean is how persuasively the meaning is being displayed and held.

When a poem's rhythm is right, the body is saying to the head, Good job, you haven't falsified my role in this enterprise.

After the superb dance concert (Momix) the other night, I felt so elated and enlarged that I knew what I should expect of poetry readings.

"Sometimes," said Whitey Ford, the great Yankee curveballer, "you need to put one right down the middle." He was speaking of surprises. I've always thought that poets, especially abstruse poets, could profit by his remark.

I dream of an art so transparent that you can look through and see the world. – Stanley Kunitz

Finally, what I want from poetry is akin to what Flaubert wanted from novels. He thought they should make us dream. I want a poem, through its precisions and accuracies, to make me remember what I know, or what I might have known if I hadn't been constrained by convention or habit.

In a sense, my father was a Willy Loman. He was my introduction to the pathetic and to sadness and heroism. I don't know how I escaped Biff's escapism, his self-destructiveness. But I did. Perhaps it was because when things went bad I still had the esteem of the schoolyard. For a long important while I didn't have to think, except as an athlete does. I just played ball. Sweet moves and the ball in the hole. The pure poetry that satisfies when you're young.

My maternal grandfather's name was Montefiore Fleischman. He was a storyteller, a lover of women, and depending on how many mistakes we allow someone before his stature is lessened, perhaps a great man. He had the kind of large personality that sometimes can tolerably house even a major flaw. In his sixties, he read a novel and drank a bottle of gin every night. Arthritic, it was how he achieved sleep.

The erotics of memory. — Joyce Carol Oates

He remembered a great deal, but the memory was uninteresting, tedious, and he was even a little annoyed at its tenacity. — Anita Brookner

The invented person, borrowed from the real — abstracted, isolated — is the person we finally know, or feel we know. I make myself up from everything I am, or could be. For many years I was more desire than fact. When I stop becoming, that's when I worry.

Too many poets are insufficiently interested in story. Their poems could be improved if they gave in more to the strictures of fiction: the establishment of a clear dramatic situation, and a greater awareness that first-person narrators are also characters and must be treated as such by their authors. The true lyric poet, of course, is exempt from this. But many poets wrongly think they are lyric poets.

I hate good taste. Those who say they have it exhibit its opposite.

As Kafka put it, there is an infinite amount of hope, but not for us. This statement really contains Kafka's hope; it is the source of his radiant serenity. — Walter Benjamin

The world, finally, tries to rob us in lots of ways. I like poems to do a bit of taking back for us. — Terry Blackhawk

Fall seven times, stand up eight. — Japanese proverb

Edward Hopper said that "painting will have to deal more fully and less obliquely with life and nature's phenomena before it can again become great." So will poetry. Yet that won't be enough. It will require compositional skills and angles of vision equal to Hopper's.

The tyranny of the actual begins. — Philip Roth

The highway is the road most people travel, often obliviously. I like going off onto the side roads, getting lost a little, finding my way back. This is how to better appreciate the highway. The mysteries of the side roads interest me, but the mysteries of the main road interest me more. I'd like my work to be the eyes and ears of such traveling.

Lovers are unreliable witnesses, which is why reliability is not always to be desired.

Mickey Rivers, a former Yankee center fielder, when asked if he was worried about being traded, said something I try to remember to live by when things are going bad. "Ain't no sense in worrying about things you got control over, 'cause if you got control over them, ain't no sense in worrying. And there ain't no sense worrying about things you got no control over, 'cause if you got no control over them, ain't no sense worrying."

Lewis Hyde's book *The Gift* made me, for a while, more generous. For about two weeks, I wanted to give everything away. Barry Lopez's book *Arctic Dreams*, equally moral and powerful, made me want to write graceful yet heavily freighted sentences. I value both books, but I'll return more often to *Arctic Dreams*.

I don't think I'd complain if I were overrated.

I believe everything you tell me, but I know that it will all turn out differently. — Henry Miller

I don't trust people until I know what they love. If they cannot admit to what they love, or in fact love nothing, I cannot take even their smartest criticisms seriously.

Can I change myself with some discoloration, that unclearness I despise in the work of other men? And what should I avoid? Anything contrived. Anything less than vital. — John Cheever

Summertime, the children older now, seventeen and twenty, their noise more quiet than in the past, but noise nonetheless. I realize how comforting those sounds are, the sounds that for years I complained about and worked to. I should admit it, silence has given me more trouble than my children have, though I love silence. Tonight, here in my room, something will come, I'm confident, the old music of my children outside my room; working music.

⚜

Touching the Leper's Hand:
Possibilities of Affirmation

*Man is a luminous pause between two great
mysteries, which yet are one.*

C.G. JUNG

A PERSON SCRUPULOUS ABOUT LANGUAGE THESE DAYS WOULD NOT
say "Have a nice day." It's the reflexive, unfelt response to almost every
one of our transactions. As language goes, it has entered the realm of the
dead. Poems that affirm too easily, that would have us accept simplifi-
cations of our feelings about experience and the world, are "Have a nice
day" poems. We cannot trust their speakers. A typical Hallmark card
verse, to offer an obvious example, falsifies our emotional life, which in
fact might be its major appeal. I found one at the stationery store that
ended with "Love is forever, / Love is you." We know that a grown-up
wrote those lines, and most likely wasn't embarrassed. And we can as-
sume that the audience for them is much larger than the audience, say,
for these enigmatic lines from David Ignatow's "Rescue the Dead":

> To love is to be led away
> into a forest where the secret grave
> is dug, singing, praising darkness
> under the trees.

Ignatow's lines suggest that at the very least, there are complicated
undercurrents to loving, and he offers us "singing" and "praising" in a
context that compels us to think about those words anew. He's rescued
those words from banality, the banality in which the "Have a nice day"
crowd finds comfort.

My favorite response to "Have a nice day" was given by a friend's seventy-five-year-old no-nonsense mother. She said, "Thank you, but I have other plans." I could trust someone who'd say that, provided that that someone wasn't a perpetual wiseguy. It has in it an appropriate disdain, a sense of phrasing, and of course wit and intelligence. If that someone were then to say something positive, I'd be disposed to yield to it.

Affirmative poetry, as such, is not of much interest. But affirmation *in* poetry is, in part, because it's so difficult to achieve. With a few exceptions, in order to be credible the poem must signify that its author is sufficiently cognizant that the world is difficult, harsh, often disappointing. The poem must in some way contain the shadow side of its affirmation.

For most of us, the intent is not to affirm, but to be true to. If we attempt to be true to the state of things, to the state of ourselves as agents in the state of things, let our attitudes fall where they may. Fidelity to experience and to one's vision is what matters most. And of course affirmation comes in many guises. Who's to say, for example, that passionate and intelligent negation isn't an affirmative act? Obviously if we are nothing but affirmative, we are liars and untrustworthy.

Some subjects lend themselves to the affirmative more readily than others. We can always sing of "The body electric" because the local, the immediate, can be credibly known and asserted. But if at the same time we sing of America with unbounded optimism we, at best, are in the wrong century. At worst, we are blind and deaf.

The lyric is the most common kind of affirmative poem. At its most celebratory it is a song of inexperience, which is not necessarily to devaluate it. It is a different achievement to write a meditative affirmative poem, which allows and involves reflection about experience. Similarly, we expect measured attitudes from any poem that's retrospective. She has fallen off the pedestal. He has revealed the less savory sides of himself. The past joy may be extolled, but there's usually a "but" soon to appear. To be affirmative when there's a "but" is no easy task.

Certainly the affirmative poems that interest me are those which affirm while acknowledging failure, limitation — the recognizable undersides of experience. "After such knowledge, what forgiveness?" Eliot writes in "Gerontion." His great question speaks to the heart of the issue. In *full* knowledge some poets are still able to affirm. Gerard

Manley Hopkins's "God's Grandeur" is one such poem. Hopkins is not naive about the world in which God's grandeur exists. In the octave of his sonnet, after saying "The world is charged with the grandeur of God," he presents a world despoiled by man:

> Generations have trod, have trod, have trod;
> And all is smeared with trade; bleared, smeared with toil;
> And wears man's smudge and shares man's smell: the soil
> Is bare now, nor can foot feel, being shod.

"And all for this," the sestet begins, "nature is never spent. / There lives the dearest freshness deep down things." The poet is trustworthy in at least two ways. He does not pretty up the world he wishes to affirm, and he finds vital language for both his complaint and his euphoria. One might say that the poem's vivifying language is in itself a testimony to lifefulness and grandeur, certainly a testimony to the poet's conviction. Moreover, the criticisms in the octave facilitate the complexity of affirmation in the last two lines of the poem. The Holy Ghost "broods" over the "bent world," but "with warm breast and with ah! bright wings." These lines are a paradigm for affirmation at its sometimes best, the negative embraced though not canceled by the positive.

Most of what is thought and observed in any given time needs to be negated. The minds we trust distrust much of what they encounter; if they are first-rate minds they also offer us that which we can value. One of the things that poetry does is to confer value, or point toward it. But it's rarely so simple as just an act of the mind. "In a dark time the eye begins to see," Roethke reminds us. Poets often are driven or drawn to what's of value by the absence of it, specifically in their own lives. They enact the journeys for us; they need not be advocates, as Hopkins was.

A poet who is often an advocate is Adrienne Rich. But in "Diving into the Wreck" she takes us on a metaphorical journey without promulgating a course of action. I won't quote that much anthologized poem in its entirety, but will risk a rough paraphrase for the purposes of my argument. "First having read the book of myths," the speaker puts on "the absurd flippers / the grave and awkward mask" to dive alone (unlike Cousteau "with his assiduous team") to "explore the wreck." The wreck, we sense, is the culture itself, whose myths and stories insufficiently include the speaker. The journey is urgent because she needs to see the wreck firsthand, "not the story of the wreck." She has undertaken this dive "to see the damage that was done / and the treasures that prevail." When she gets to the wreck she's suddenly androgynous, "the mermaid whose dark hair / streams black, the merman in his armored body ... we are the half-destroyed instruments / that once held to a course ..." This is a powerful and telling juncture in the poem, and a suggestion that at the heart of the wreck we are — women and men — in it together. But it is of course the woman, driven by necessity, who has made the journey, who has had to negate in order to possibly affirm. Correctly, I think, she's unable to affirm at the end of this exploratory dive. The poem ends like this:

> We are, I am, you are
> by cowardice or courage
> the one who find our way
> back to this scene
> carrying a knife, a camera
> a book of myths
> in which
> our names do not appear.

The use of the pronouns may annoy, and the conclusion certainly doesn't offer us or the speaker any solace, but I would say that the enactment of the journey itself — in its dangerous searching and witnessing — is an act of affirmation. She has her knife (to cut into) and her camera (to record) the wreck. In any great journey there is travail and difficulty before there is improvement. Rich is wise about the conditions she creates in her poem.

Most of us make half-journeys. That is why the Christs, the Buddhas, the Martin Luther Kings, *and* the significant poets are often frightening when they enact for us what it means to complete a gesture. All the people I admire have gone further than I'm either willing or able to go. They attract and repel. If you go down into the wreck, as Rich's life attests, you must change your life. And thus your poetry. Destruction can be a form of creation.

Love poems are, historically, affirmative territory. It would seem of little value to declaim that love makes us feel good. Often it's like saying the sun is out when the sun is out. But we will do so over and over until the end of time. We cannot help ourselves – not a bad motive for poetry. If our language is fresh, those who care will pay proper attention. If the poem aspires to song, as Burns's "A Red, Red Rose" does, we might forgive its simple sentiments.

The affirmation in love poems that I most admire comes from different sources. Better that somebody loving us might make us feel ambivalent or even unworthy, or that our entire history of loving makes love somewhat problematical. That's the content that might disturb the Hallmark audience. The wonderful ending of Robert Hayden's "Those Winter Sundays" is indicative "What did I know, what did I know / of love's austere and lonely offices?" I remember first reading those lines many years ago. I was affected by them in the context of the poem, yes, but I recall feeling oddly elated by Hayden's suggestion that love could be austere and lonely. Maybe one aspect of affirmation in poetry occurs when a poem offers language for our inarticulate understandings. It affirms what we vaguely already knew, makes us less strange to ourselves, invites us more fully into the human fold.

In my formative twenties I saw each Ingmar Bergman film as it came along. Everyone I knew called the films depressing, even if they liked them. Though the subject matter, arguably, was depressing, I always left the theater elated, charged up. I know now that it had something to do with appreciation of artistry, but even more so with Bergman's ability to take on the gravest concerns with a steady hand and eye. In Wallace Stevens's terms, he made his imagination mine. Does one feel depressed when he or she looks at "Guernica"? Or when one finishes any of the great tragedies? When I first read Kinnell's *Book of Nightmares*, though I was fully aware of the subject matter, I experienced the intense pleasure of being in the presence of embodied language. Later, when I heard him read it, I felt like smiling all the way through, and I hope I did. In addition to the language I was responding to an evocation of spirit. That the subject matter was grave made that spirit all the more compelling and, might I say, heartening. Dylan Thomas concludes "Fern Hill" with

> Oh, as I was young and easy in the mercy of his means
> Time held me green and dying

Though I sang in my chains like the sea.

In spite of and perhaps because of their chains, the great singers sing. Thomas said of his poetry, "It is the record of my individual struggle from darkness toward some measure of light." And I would argue that any good poem is some measure of light. The light is always affirmative; what it is illuminating may not be. Moreover, we must remember that poetry — and all that deserves to be called art — is larger than its subject matter. The beautifully made object has a light of its own.

A friend of mine, a poet, joined the Peace Corps at age seventy, and has been in Africa the last few years. One of his letters to me was about lepers begging in the streets, and how he would give them money, but avert his eyes. Gradually he learned not to avert his eyes. He allowed himself to be pleased with himself, but then realized that when he put the money in their hands he was careful not to touch their hands. In this case he knew that true charity involved touching as well. Or perhaps that touching was the true giving. In his most recent letter, he said he was still working on that.

Look for what must be overcome or transcended and we'll find the possibility of the deepest affirmations. Affirmation of what? That which exists just beyond or beneath the satisfactory, the acceptable. With luck and some wisdom that's where we might find that the authentic resides. The authentic is that which must be found or located, either inside or outside oneself. It's clear that one must pay one's dues in order to find it. With poets, there are craft as well as experiential dues. As a *maker* of poems, the poet must be ready for the important subject.

Here are the last several lines of "Healing the Mare," a poem by Linda McCarriston that I will send to my friend in Africa. The poem introduces a mare with festering sores, and the speaker says,

> … I bathe you
> and see your coat returning,
> your deep force surfacing in a
> new layer of hide: black wax
> alive against weather and flies.

But this morning, misshapen
still, you look like an effigy,
something rudely made, something
made to be buffeted, or like
an old comforter — are they both
one in the end? So both a child

and a mother, with my sponge and
my bucket, I come to anoint, to
anneal the still weeping, to croon
you *baby, poor baby* for the sake
of the song, to polish you up,
for the sake of the touch, to a shine.

As I soothe you I surprise wounds
of my own this long time unmothered.
As you stand, scathed and scabbed,
with your head up, I swab. As you
press, I lean into my own loving
touch, for which no wound
is too ugly.

In the act of healing the mare, the speaker finds "wounds / of my own this long time unmothered." Isn't this the poem and the poet's first discovery, made possible by placing herself in proximity to the malodorous sores? This is nothing new as an emblem for what can be generative in art. One thinks of Philoctetes and his wound, as Edmund Wilson discussed him and it in *The Wound and the Bow*, the wound facilitating the significant act. But it feels authentic in McCarriston's poem, and leads to a deepening. "As you / press, I lean into my own loving / touch for which no wound / is too ugly." This is hard-won affirmation, born out of correlatives in the self, that I suspect my friend in Africa is seeking. Maybe he needs to know that what he wants to give is not charity, in the conventional sense of that word. Rather, it has something to do with self-healing. One must be impelled by powerful, often unconscious imperatives in order to complete a difficult gesture. I suspect that the affirmative poems to which I'm most drawn evolve from such imperatives.

I don't wish to suggest that affirmation in poetry must always arise from darkness. But it helps if the poet demonstrates he or she is savvy about it. Savvy enough that the beneficent wish (as in Auden's famous elegy for Yeats) contain sufficient bite.

> In the desert of the heart
> Let the healing fountain start,
> In the prison of his days
> Teach the free man how to praise.

The desert and the prison — these emblems of travail and difficulty — are the very sources of possible affirmation, just as they are equally the sources of, say, the blues. In this luminous pause between two great mysteries, it should not bother us that the sources are the same.

※

Poets, Poetry, and the Spiritual

> *I am willing to leave God out of the matter, since I*
> *personally find no words to qualify or invoke that*
> *name. But I am unwilling to leave the spirit out...*
> *as much an issue of nihilism as belief. A great writer*
> *may deny meaning to spirit — witness Kafka, Beckett*
> *— but we think it vulgar and vapid if he do so with-*
> *out a trace of despair; and we note how often he*
> *returns to deny.*
>
> IHAB HASSAN

> *It is always an invisible belief that sustains the*
> *edifice of our sensory world and deprived of which*
> *it totters.*
>
> MARCEL PROUST

WHEN IT COMES TO SPIRITUALITY, I, LIKE IHAB HASSAN, AM WILLING to leave God out of the matter. But not necessarily the *idea* of God, which ever since I gave up Catholicism in my late teens I've felt free to contemplate. To contemplate the idea of God is inevitably to become fascinated by the cross-cultural sacred texts that embody this insistent idea and the collective psychology that can be inferred from them. "Heart and mind continue to cry out to hell, to heaven, for something more," Hassan says, and concludes: "The cry is hopeless, its very hopelessness indistinguishable from hope on the other side of despair." Because I concur with him, I begin by admitting that, to me, celestial hopelessness is earthly opportunity, a challenge to our capacity to endure and give meaning to our lives. The despair I sometimes feel has more to do with the vileness of the daily news and my ineffectuality in regard to it than it does with cosmic meaninglessness. I try not to let either defeat me. I know that despair often can be a ticket to an unchosen journey, and to survive it is to come back with glimpses of what was not available to us before. Yet one would be a fool not to seek despair's antidotes, joy and good work, and try to live in the sensual world among "the ten thousand thousand" things. I also seek those poems and stories that address what's most difficult and elusive about our experience, correlatives to the nether regions of our feelings and apprehensions. In them perhaps is the greatest solace, evidence that we're not alone, and no doubt where some of what we mean by "spiritual" resides.

For years I've held dear Paul Eluard's statement, "There is another world and it is in this one." It has been my credo as a poet. I take as a given of my job the need to enact and deliver both worlds, which involves giving voice to interiorities and evanescences and to the surfaces that conceal and evoke them. In fact, though, when I write I rarely think about such things; mostly I'm just trying to work my subject, worry it home, give it shape. I know that without form and the sounds that inspirit it, our keenest insights are little more than excerpts from Bartlett's. Our poems must read and sound as if we inhabit them, and one way we do is with our measured breath (*spiritus*), a component of voice: Pitched just right, voice reveals the spirit behind it, which is part of what we receive when we take in a poem's content.

Wallace Stevens deals with this directly in "The Idea of Order at Key West." He presents a woman, his poetic surrogate, who "sang beyond the genius of the sea." "Whose spirit is this? we said, because we knew / It was the spirit that we sought and knew / that we should ask this often as she sang." Everytime we're compelled by a voice, we ask this question. Later we're told that "It was her voice that made / The sky acutest at its vanishing. She measured to the hour its solitude." These are perceptions of aural and phrasal delicacy in a poem that throughout is itself onomatopoeic evidence of what it is interested in. It's an *ars poetica*, one of the many that Stevens would write. The voice and the qualities we can divine from it are inextricably part of the overt subject

—in this case a woman singing about the sea—because it is Stevens' voice and the spirit behind it we most listen to. Its last stanza further points to Stevens' poetics:

> Oh! Blessed rage for order, pale Ramon,
> The maker's rage to order words of the sea,
> Words of the fragrant portals, dimly-starred,
> And of ourselves and of our origins,
> In ghostlier demarcations, keener sounds.

Rage *for* order. Words that sing of us and our origins *and* make the finest distinctions. I love the implication that composition, however orderly, should be a passionate enterprise, that a vibrant order isn't made by those disposed to mere neatness, and that shades of meaning are achieved with all the tools the poet has at his disposal. Stevens is one of our great musicians of the spirit, exemplifying in this poem and in others that voice and its music are part of what constitutes content. His masterpiece "Sunday Morning" does the same, and perhaps best offers us a version of paradise that is nothing more or less than the sensuous, secular world.

But voice, finally, is mysterious; it can't be willed and often is driven by unconscious forces. Witness Kafka's little prose poem "The Sirens."

> These are the seductive voices of the night; the Sirens,
> too, sang that way. It would be doing them an injustice to
> think that they wanted to seduce; they knew they had
> claws and sterile wombs, and they lamented this aloud.
> They could not help it if their laments sounded so beautiful.

TR. BY CLEMENT GREENBERG

Certain poets, like the Sirens or, say, like singers Bessie Smith and Billie Holiday, can't keep their lives out of their voices. We listen to their words, yes, but mostly we're listening to *them*, to something their voices carry and conceal. We conclude we've been moved, spoken to, but what we've experienced is something necessary being played out that has found something needy in us. "Beautiful" is a conflation of the two.

Eluard's "other world in this one" points to where the spiritual might be located. But I must confess that I've experienced nothing of the spiritual in any of its familiar theological usages. I've had a few experiences that I'd call sublime, each one rooted in conditions brought about by someone's art or someone's flesh. Each made me quiet, grateful, maybe for a while enraptured. I hesitate to make a greater claim for them.

What constitutes a spiritual experience? Seemingly, these days, almost anything. Cooking a meal, hiking, tuning an engine – we're told – can still the mind and awaken in us a sense of the numinous. This may be so for advanced practitioners in certain traditions, who through intense discipline have bridged the secular / sacred, the quotidian / spiritual. A practitioner of Soto Zen, for example, says, "What are my miraculous powers? Hauling wood, carrying water," and lives in daily accordance with that awareness. But in cultures with theologies that concern themselves with the Divine, it seems to me that to have *many* spiritual experiences is to regularize what should be rarefied. It shouldn't be surprising that in our New Age times *awesome* is the word most trivialized by young people. They use it as a synonym for *good* and they use it often. Awe (how many have ever experienced it?) produces stunned silence, which indicates that spiritual experiences resist the language that might describe them. If in our poems we choose to engage what might be spiritual, we therefore need to be conscious of silence, perhaps try to approximate it. This is among poetry's paradoxical burdens – to limn and deliver the unsayable, sometimes even to let the white space around our words do some invisible work for us.

The experiences one claims to have had with God or gods, like the ones poets claim to have with a "muse," what else can these be except heightened conversations with oneself? The believer, transported, gives God his words which then become His words. The poet (who could be a believer too) thanks the muse for creations he cannot reconcile as having come wholly from himself. Not as readily acknowledged are the demons that inhabit the same psychic territory, crying out defiant *No's* to our easy affirmations, or appearing as images – rough, slouching beasts – which complicate and startle. That's why people who profess connections to the spirit world are sometimes disturbing, and why the unconscious has been dangerous terrain for some poets. Poets are not far removed from, say, prophets and shamans who believe into existence what they intuit. If poets are somewhat rescued from the dark side of what they locate, it's because they're linguistically manipulative, technically dexterous, in love with achieved effects. But as they write they long to forget for a while that they are makers, long for those moments when they are tripped into registering sensation and experience with an unlegislated eye.

Poets resist the debasement of language and the easily-made claims of their culture, and know the insufficiency of the rational. If philosophers tend to demystify, poets tend to make forays into the mysterious without trying to tame it. Clearly, the rational will get us no further than the sanctioned, fixed boundaries proscribed by societies that want order but not the rage for it. I've recently come to feel that Stevens, for example, is a wild para-rational poet, as wild, say, as Ginsberg. The insurance executive and "The Emperor of Ice Cream"—amazing. Every time Stevens sat down to write he must have left behind the spirit of his insurance office, entered into another spirit entirely.

The spirit that's in voice, that comes from the entire wherewithal of a person, is one aspect of the spiritual. The spirit that seems to come from outside of the person is another. Though I've speculated that when one attempts to engage such a spirit the result is a heightened conversation with oneself, I don't want to say that a spirit-world exterior to oneself doesn't exist. My two experiences with ghosts persuade me that it does. I'm also persuaded by auras that great men and women give off, which in more acceptable societal language might be called charisma. Isn't a halo an artist's representation of a felt, if not actually perceived, extra dimension? I've known people to see the equivalent of a halo when a great yoga master came into a room. They talk of his body's blueness.

Though such things may be just a tiny part of what Eluard means by the other world, we can imagine that our ancestors regularly lived among spirits both palpable and imagined—emanations they felt but couldn't account for. Everything that befell them had a spiritual cause. The poets and storytellers, driven by necessity and fear, created Hell, Valhalla, reincarnation, Paradise—the myths by which the terrifying world was made livable. They *still* create the world, though of course they are listened to with less urgency. What is the new supreme fiction? Is it nonfiction? The illusion of fact—as seen in memoir, autobiography? The salvation that technology promises to the technological? Of course there is no supreme fiction, only little fictions that offer us little truths. I love the people who still read poetry as if that's where some of the news is, lonely for combinations of words that delight, or properly disturb, or plumb the ineffable, or give voice to their unarticulated lives.

Before self-consciousness, gods and demons spoke and had to be consulted. Even with our psychological sophistication, self-conscious-ness remains as mysterious as a god whispering in one's ear. Yet to know that something like it exists goes a long way toward delimiting a God-driven universe and helping us separate what is real from what is imag-ined. Shamans and so-called witch doctors may have been the first to have had a glimmer of it, the intuitive ones who recognized a connec-tion between revelation and their own powers. But poor Young Good-man Brown, to choose a fictional representation of someone not gifted with self-consciousness, was tormented by "sinful" thoughts that he had no way of knowing were normal. In his dream he went out into the woods and met the Devil, and he brought all the good people of his town with him, even his aptly-named wife Faith. Jung helps us here with his concept that people unaware of their shadow side will project it onto others, but Hawthorne clearly understood that concept before Jung, as did all the great writers from Sophocles to Shakespeare to Dostoyevski, who have forged the way for the great psychologists. It would seem that as we have been made more visible to ourselves our behavior would have changed. But no, we just *know* more. Most of us are still are out in some forest with our demons, still bringing them home.

So far, in addition to poets, I've mentioned playwrights, novelists, story-tellers, and psychologists. But for the purposes of this essay they are all poets, cousins in the enterprise. They are the artisans whose de-votion to craft and discipline has brought them to places where the un-available becomes available. In their greatest moments, what they see is related to the clarities the yogi perceives in the eighth stage, or what the physicist sees at the moment an unseen order becomes seen. Process has gotten them there, some discovery or other compositional élan trip-ping them into unselfconsciousness. They're flying. They've written some things they didn't know they knew. Exhilarating? Perhaps, but my experience tells me that at that moment they're still worrying their poems forward, or debating whether a comma would be better than a dash, or wondering how to reconcile the calm beginning with the wild-ness they've just produced. Satisfaction, if ever, comes later.

Stevens defines the imagination as "the power of the mind over the possibilities of things." The faithful and the innocent call such power *God*. Others of us feel that, whatever it is, it has occurred because we've put ourselves in a place (say, the quiet room where we write) where we can be visited by ourselves and maybe make a few loose ends cohere. Of course, included in the possibilities of things are assorted evils, the nay alongside the yea, the despoiled world next to the luscious one, everything that complicates our ability to have certainties. The imagination that entertains a God has much to accommodate.

"Somewhere in the world / is the secret name / for God, many-lettered, unpronounceable," I've said in a poem. That name will never be found, and shouldn't be. It's not enough to omit the *o* in God, though the intention is right. By choosing to confound the One Name we preserve the mystery it stands for and open ourselves to a many-ness.

Poetry is Adamic, plumbing the ineffable as it names the birds and the trees and the lives we endure behind closed doors. The poet, in order to be wonderful, needs to be full of wonder and a kind of scientific poise. Nothing, no matter how small, should be unworthy of his gaze, his investigatory spirit. Jane Hirshfield writes, "Again the holy striving / has given way / to ordinary joy." Hopkins says, "Glory be to God for dappled things — " and goes on to praise "All things counter, original, spare, strange." Ann Lauterbach advocates "A constant dialectics of engagement." In each of these passages, there's the suggestion that attention to one thing will lead to attention to another, maybe even its opposite, and that perhaps all opposites are kindred, part of what *is*. The world, properly seen, is vital, various, contradictory. As Hirshfield suggests, the pursuit of the ineffable may lead us into a radiant dailiness. Similarly, the naming of what's around us may lead us toward consideration of the ineffable.

Here is a possible definition of spirituality in poetry: what exists in the intimations we (as readers) feel as the poet finds language and music for what he leans toward but doesn't know. Gary Snyder says it this way:

HOW POETRY COMES TO ME

It comes blundering over the
Boulders at night, it stays
Frightened outside the

> Range of my campfire
> I go to meet it at the
> Edge of the light

That kind of gestalt — the subject moving toward the poet, the poet go-
ing out to meet it — is of course a romanticizing of how poetry occurs,
accurate only in broad terms. Most poets would argue that, for them,
the next line should be, "And then we revise a lot." But Snyder in other
poems shows his respect for the physical world, as if he knows that pro-
found intimations are more often given off when the poet has sought
precision rather than vision. The visionary / spiritual poet, we can be
sure, keeps a clear eye on the boulders and the campfire.

Yet the visionary can be achieved by more abstract means as well, if
those means are grounded in the recognizable world. Witness Emily
Dickinson:

> The Brain — is wider than the Sky —
> For — put them side by side —
> The one the other will contain —
> With Ease — and You — beside
>
> The Brain is deeper than the sea —
> For — hold them — Blue to Blue —
> The one the other will absorb —
> As Sponges — Buckets — do —
>
> The Brain is just the weight of God —
> For — Heft them — Pound for Pound —
> And they will differ — if they do —
> As Syllable from Sound —

With her incisive equation between mind and God, Dickinson works
against the Christian orthodoxies of her time, yet a fair reader need not
conclude that God is reduced by this association with the human brain.
On the contrary, God retains his capaciousness. Dickinson, however, is
interested in ideas more than in reverence. Argument by analogy is the
poem's method. Sky and sea give us almost infinite dimensions, while
the surprising and enigmatic distinction between syllable and sound
tests and teases us while preserving mystery.

Modernism, of which Dickinson is one of the precursors, confounded our certainties, our wonder, and then offered us fragments to shore up against our ruins. Or offered us fragments, without solace, often beautiful in themselves. We learned to develop a tolerance for the discordant, the fractured, the splash of paint, the non sequitur; they seemed to have something to do with the real.

Compositionally — painters, musicians, and poets — conferred value or the absence of it by broken means. Picasso. Stravinsky. Williams. There was a new secular spirit in the air, a new vision, yet somehow the idea of God and the need for prayer didn't die. Philip Larkin, who resisted the modernists, may have signified why. In "Church Going," a poem of religious ambivalence, his wry and hesitant speaker moves from "awkward reverence" to imagining churches as future archaeological curiosities, to this surprising affirmation:

> It pleases me to stand in silence here;
>
> A serious house on serious earth it is,
> In whose blent air all our compulsions meet,
> Are recognised, and robed as destinies.
> And that much can never be obsolete,
> Since someone will forever be surprising
> A hunger in himself to be more serious,
> and gravitating with it to this ground,
> Which, he once heard, was proper to grow wise in,
> If only that so many dead lie round.

Still, for me the truest poems of spirit do not directly take on religion or religious issues as such. James Wright's "The Jewel" has always invited me into it, offered a heightened intuition of the numinous.

> There is this cave
> In the air behind my body
> That nobody is going to touch:
> A cloister, a silence
> Closing around a blossom of fire.
> When I stand upright in the wind,
> My bones turn to dark emeralds.

I first read this as a surreal poem, brave in its strange and unqualified assertions. To the extent that I "understood" it or even wished such a reductiveness, it was a poem that evoked a kind of fierce integrity; I have a secret place, the speaker was asserting, and it's so peculiarly mine that it glows. Integrity. Aura. Spirit. Could these be interchangable? Something in Wright, we feel, needed to select its own society. Recently, reading this poem to a friend, one of the people I know who has the most heightened intuitions—I was nevertheless startled when she said that Wright's cave was personal to her; that she intimately knew the place. To her it was a realistic poem. Santayana wrote, "Spirit chills the flesh and is itself on fire." Was Wright speaking about spirit in that sense? Surely "my bones turn to dark emeralds" is suggestive of it.

W.S Merwin's "For The Anniversary Of My Death" is another poem infused with a quality both mysterious and recognizable.

> Every year without knowing it I have passed the day
> When the last fires will wave to me
> And the silence will set out
> Tireless traveler
> Like the beam of a lightless star
> Then I will no longer
> Find myself in life as in a strange garment
> Surprised at the earth
> And the love of one woman
> And the shamelessness of men
> As today writing after three days of rain
> Hearing the wren sing and the falling cease
> And bowing not knowing to what

What to say except there's a familiar strangeness to this poem, the consciousness behind it so sentient and quiescent that it seems to enact for us something just beneath or beyond our grasp, to invoke some ignorant reverence that we nevertheless understand. And at its end I hear that silence I referred to earlier, perhaps suggested by the absence of punctuation. I read this poem again and again with pleasure and a kind of wordless semi-understanding that feels sufficient.

The classic spiritual journey is from travail to understanding or acceptance. The structure of many poems is not dissimilar, though many poets—like Merwin—choose to conclude their poems without conclusion. Rather, conclusion is open-ended, evocative of the mysteries that the poem has enacted.

One is not tempted to commit the biographical fallacy when speaking about Merwin and his poems. In fact, one of the attractions of his best creations is that they seem to arise from nowhere, with their triggering mechanism concealed or suppressed. But when we discuss some poets' work, biography seems to matter, or at least should not be ignored. Anna Akhmatova is such a poet — her husband executed by the Bolsheviks in 1921, her work officially banned from publication in 1925, her long endurance under Stalinism during which many of her friends were murdered or driven to suicide. I think her two poems that follow are strong in their own right, yet stronger if we know their historical context. In comparison, the American poets I've been citing had the fortune and misfortune of writing poems that are not accentuated by severe national circumstances.

> Everything is plundered, betrayed, sold,
> Death's great black wing scrapes the air,
> Misery gnaws to the bone.
> Why then do we not despair?
>
> By day, from the surrounding woods,
> cherries blow summer into town;
> at night the deep transparent skies
> glitter with new galaxies.
>
> And the miraculous comes so close
> to the ruined, dirty houses —
> something not known to anyone at all,
> but wild in our breast for centuries.

> 1921, TR. BY STANLEY KUNITZ WITH MAX
> HAYWARD, FROM *Anno Domini*

SUMMER GARDEN

I want to visit the roses
In that lonely
Park where the statues remember me young

And I remember them under the water
Of the Neva. In that fragrant quiet
Between the lines of Tsarskoye I hear
A creak of masts. And the swan swims
Still, admiring its lovely
Double. And a hundred thousand steps,
Friend and enemy, enemy and friend,
Sleep. Endless is the procession of shades
Between the granite vase and palace door.
There my white nights
Whisper of someone's discreet exalted
Love.
And everything is mother-
Of-pearl and jasper,
But the light's source is a secret.

1959, JULY, LENINGRAD, TR. BY
D.M. THOMAS

Behind each poem is despair or the specter of it, and in each resides evidence of the difficult struggle against that despair. "And the miraculous comes so close / to the ruined, dirty houses —," she says in the 1921 poem. "Close" is a wonderful choice by the translators, heartbreaking almost, suggestive of the world's beauty in the stanza above it, but also of whatever mysterious sustaining spirit exists that permits people to endure great hardship. Note that it's "wild in *our* breast for centuries," which reminds us that the poem has been a "we" poem all along. Akhmatova attempts to speak for the Russian people, not just the individual sufferer.

The 1959 poem is more overtly personal, but structurally it's not much different from the first. It negotiates memory and longing, the loveliness of the remembered details ghost-haunted throughout. Both poems detail the daily pleasures that allow one to live with hardship, and both suggest that something mysterious and ethereal is a sustaining force, too.

Spirituality in poetry. Here's another attempt at a definition: A journey through travail toward an understanding that leads back to mystery.

I would be remiss if I didn't cite poems that take us into and through the dark night of the soul, even ones that might leave us there.

Can there be spirituality in negation? Need solace always arise out of good news? Yeats wrote, "I shall find the dark grow luminous, the void fruitful when I understand I have nothing." Ihab Hassan, whom I quoted at the outset, says "Sooner or later, all roads of spiritual exploration lead to the crux of nihilism," by which he means that faith is tested by realizing that there might be nothing to inspire it. I attest to having felt something like spiritual solace when Frost says he is "absent-spirited" and avers that he's afraid of his own "desert places." Or when Roethke's "on a Dark Time" wonders fearfully, "Which I is I?" Or when in "Gerontion" Eliot asks, "After such knowledge, what forgiveness?" I've felt it in Ginsburg's restorative "Howl." In Jeffers' many ferocities. These are the solaces of recognition, my half-thoughts and feelings finding companions and words.

Ted Hughes is the modern poet who most chillingly and unredemptively enters the existential void, my void, and conjures the dark forces that might haunt it. His 1971 book *Crow* offers anything but solace, and yet many of its poems should be considered in the realm of the spiritual. The demon part of the realm. His personified Crow is emblematic of an omnipresent emptiness and dread, the absence of value, our atrocious daily news.

To a Buddhist, he (Crow) is simply part of what is, but in Western traditions in which the focus is on a personal God, the fact of Crow is a spiritual test. Hughes makes Crow so negatively powerful that we understand why someone might doubt the presence and beneficence of God. In "Crow Alights," for example,

> He saw the stars, fuming away into black, mushrooms of the
>   nothing forest, clouding their spores, the virus of God.
> And he shivered with the horror of Creation...

> Crow blinked...

> He stared at the evidence.
> Nothing escaped him. (Nothing could escape.)

In "Crow Blacker than Ever" we are told that

> Man couldn't be man nor God God.

The agony

Grew.

Crow

Grinned

Crying: "This is my Creation",
Flying the black flag of himself.

In lieu of a God who can't be God and amid we who can't even be our-
selves, Crow is happy to fly the black flag of himself. Nothing escaped
him, Hughes asserts, and nothing could. These serious puns suggest
that "nothing" is his province, and that he fills voids with the nothing he
is. Crow will always be there when belief falters, and indeed Hughes
knows that the twentieth century is evidence enough that belief in our
humanity is as difficult to maintain as a belief in God. In Hughes' uni-
verse, Crow is everywhere. For us to share his pessimism a leap of faith
is hardly necessary.

But of course Hughes is writing poetry, not metaphysical tracts. His
"Crow" poems constitute a system of language through which aspects
of existence are rendered and framed for our examination. Fundamen-
tally, they are not unlike poems that attempt to praise and exalt; they are
formalized intuitions into the way things are. As my student Jeremy
Stevens has reminded me, at the highest levels of thought a distinction
may not exist between the spiritual and the aesthetic. A poem is a rev-
elation achieved by means of words the poet finds and arranges. There
are many kinds of poems with different linguistic strategies and ambi-
tions, but to me language successfully arranged to evoke the mysteries
of the world is sacred. Memorable language inevitably becomes part of
what we call reality. Demons, gods, the concealed world, the world of
appearances, the language that pertains to each—are all part of the vital
conundrum. Conundrums? Hughes is one agent in the large enterprise.

I find it compelling that Akhmatova's poems are so full of the visible,
tangible world, and a secret world of light that she finds immanent. She
saw Crow, in fact lived with Crow all around her, and still figured out

how to go on. No doubt as a person she had great spiritual strength. But if the word "spiritual" in poetry has any value at all, it is in the ways the other world in this one becomes visible to us, either through suffering or through the felicities of process – the writer placing herself in a position, not necessarily at the edge but at least close to it, where she can be startled into what she didn't yet know. How then to live with such knowledge is the question; like getting in touch with oneself, apprehending what exists beyond appearances does not always result in solace. The demons of consciousness are perhaps even more frightening than the demons of unconsciousness. They're never very far from where wisdom is, and Crow is one of the demons of consciousness against which we measure our more positive beliefs.

Spirituality in poetry, most neutrally put, arises from our breath-driven, form-seeking pursuits of what is. It's probably more perceived and felt by the reader than by the poet, who inevitably has busied himself with the smallest details, as all makers do. Those details, of course, must pass hard tests for the poet, and finally must be more than details. They must constitute an arrangement of words that he or she emotionally and intellectually owns. I've rarely heard poets say that they've written a spiritual poem. They're more likely to feel they've gotten right something that seems important.

In my early, less neutral thinking about this subject, I was prepared to argue that all good poems are spiritual in that they evidence an acute attention to experience, and therefore put us – in Stevens' term – "in agreement with reality." I still hold that to be true, especially if putting us in agreement with reality means that the other world inside this one has been made manifest and thus is part of our sense of the real. But the poems I've mentioned have impelled me toward other attempts at definition. No doubt someone persuaded by any of the great religions would offer different definitions and arguments, not to mention different poems as illustrations, which is as it should be. The subject is large enough to permit many approaches. Obviously faith and devotion can lead one to profound attentiveness; I clearly prefer to be attentive to what the world looks and feels like when some of the illusions that help us live in it are stripped way.

But perhaps "clearly" isn't right. Recently I read Charles Wright's book *Black Zodiac*, which trenchantly and darkly exemplifies a fusion of an acute attention to experience *and* a longing for something more. Here's a passage from "Disjecta Membra:"

> Compulsive cameo. God's blue breath
> So light on the skin, so infinite,
>
> Why do I have to carry you, unutterable?
> Why do you shine out,
>   lost penny, unspendable thing,
>
> Irreversible, unappeasable, luminous,
> Recoursed on the far side of language?
>
> Tomorrow's our only hiding place,
> November its last address —
>   such small griefs, such capture,
>
> Insurmountable comforts.
> And still I carry you. And still you continue to shine out.

⌖

The Hand Reaching Into the Crowd: James Wright's Grace and the 1993 World Series

WE LIVE IN A GRACELESS AGE. ACCORDINGLY THE WORD GRACE (in its various parts of speech) has lost power and significance, though it is frequently used. We have our saving graces, we are graced by one's presence, we seek to be in someone's good graces, and sometimes we need grace periods, which instructively, are given these days more by banks than by other higher powers. A recent headline read, Still Cheaper Chicken May Grace Our Menus Soon. The word is nearly unhearable, nearly dead, in that contexts in which it is familiarly used rarely compel us to engage its meaning. It might be said that all much-used, debased words are looking for restoration, for revivifying contexts.

In its Latin and Old French roots the verb means either to favor or to give thanks. In Modern French it means "to pardon." James Wright's grace in "Two Poems for President Harding" has much to do with the Modern French meaning, but also with refinement of movement and elegance of proportions, and thus with the noun grace. The noun's theological definition refers to God's free and undeserved favor, at once suggestive of beneficence and selectivity. We cannot earn it; we can only hope for mercy (for the muse?). A second meaning in most American dictionaries is "to honor."

Everytime I've watched a Donahue or a Geraldo show, I've craved *grace* in any of its original meanings, high among them to honor or to pardon. In most daily encounters, too. And, always, I've thought about it in relation to my own moments of gracelessness. The word seems most genuinely alive as an adjective used to describe something physical, as in to be graceful in the ballet, or in sports. Its most genuine use as a verb is to give thanks, as in saying grace at the dinner table. In times of bountifulness or sufficiency, we hear or may have told grace-at-dinner jokes. (These can be likened to poems we may have written when nothing was at stake. Or the easy irreverence of the cynic, or merely of the philosophically and artistically young.) *Thank you,* felt beyond good manners, whether it's for God or the evening's cook, remains a lovely phrase. I think we know when to trust it. But grace suggesting pardon or forgiveness, those other Christian traits, asks more of us, and interests me more.

Wright's poem enacts such grace, as does a gesture of secular beneficence by a player on the Philadelphia Phillies after the 1993 World Series, which resulted in a poem of mine that I include here. I have in mind the interplay of deeds and the imaginations that shape them, of grace done and grace made. But also of grace given, those mysterious gifts in our poems that we have in some way (usually through years of practice) situated ourselves to receive. After all, an artist is a god of various small universes. Most of what we know of grace and gracefulness has arisen from pen, brush, chisel, camera, musical instrument, the body itself. In the case of words, not to mention The Word, some teller has always been selecting and meditating what needed to be told, though I don't mean to suggest that this is always a conscious process. But something was urging the artist forward. Necessity and grace. The latter, without the former, is mere curlicue.

James Wright's poem partially rescues Warren Harding from the cool, less empathetic judgments of history, though it doesn't attempt to question the accuracy of those judgments. By poem's end, we are persuaded to feel—because Wright has done feeling for us—what it might mean to fail and die ashamed in public. The speaker, let's say it in this instance, Wright himself, will not—for reasons the poem implies—be one who stands superior to a fellow "citizen," however disgraced.

TWO POEMS FOR PRESIDENT HARDING

One: His Death

In Marion, the honey locust trees are falling.
Everybody in town remembers the white hair,
The campaign of a lost summer, the front porch
Open to the public, and the vaguely stunned smile
Of a lucky man.

"Neighbor, I want to be helpful," he said once.
Later, "You think I'm honest, don't you?"
Weeping drunk.

I am drunk this evening in 1961,
In a jag for my countryman,
Who died of crab meat on the way back from Alaska.
Everyone knows the joke.

How many honey locusts have fallen,
Pitched rootlong into the open graves of strip mines,
Since the first World War ended
And Wilson the gaunt deacon jogged sullenly
Into silence?
Tonight,
The cancerous ghosts of old con men
Shed their leaves.
For a proud man, lost between the turnpike near Cleveland
And the chiropractor's signs looming among the dead mulberry
        trees,
There is no place left to go
But home.

"Warren lacks mentality," one of his friends said.

Yet he was beautiful, he was the snowfall
Turned to white stallions standing still
Under dark elm trees.

He died in public. He claimed the secret right
To be ashamed.

Two: His Tomb in Ohio

... he died of a busted gut.

MENCKEN, ON BRYANT

A hundred slag piles north of us,
At the mercy of the moon and rain,
He lies in his ridiculous
Tomb, our fellow citizen.
No, I have never seen that place,
Where many shadows of faceless thieves
Chuckle and stumble and embrace
On beer cans, stogie butts, and graves.

One holiday, one rainy week
After the country fell apart,
Hoover and Coolidge came to speak
And snivel about his broken heart.
His grave, a huge absurdity,
Embarrassed cops and visitors.
Hoover and Coolidge crept away
By night, and women closed their doors.

Now junkmen call their children in
Before they catch their deaths of cold;
Young lovers let the moon begin
Its quick spring; and the day grows old;
The mean one-legger who rakes up leaves
Has chased the loafers out of the park;
Minnegan Leonard half-believes
In God, and the poolroom goes dark;

America goes on, goes on
Laughing, and Harding was a fool.
Even his big pretentious stone
Lays him bare to ridicule.
I know it. But don't look at me.
By God, I didn't start this mess.
Whatever moon and rain may be,
The hearts of men are merciless.

The poems begin with the citing of Harding's birth place, Marion, where the honey locust trees are "falling," a word that commences a mood and a motif. When the fallen honey locusts are next mentioned, they are linked with "the open grave of strip mines" to suggest a denuded landscape the poet now occupies, spiritually as well as physically. The "proud man ... with no place left to go / But home" is usefully ambiguous; it could refer to either Harding or the poet. What is not ambiguous is that "home" is only slightly better than being lost between the turnpike near Cleveland and the chiropractor's signs.

Harding, of course, was a casualty of The Peter Principle; he had the misfortune of reaching the level of his incompetence. There've been several Hardings who've achieved the Presidency, but none quite so limited. His corruptions had no malice in it, no bite, nothing to hate. It never reached the interesting level of tragedy — in the Greek sense — as Nixon's did. Nixon was a bright man with some major tragic flaws. Harding was, as the poem says, a fool. He chose, and was loyal to shady, slippery friends. The Tea Pot Dome Scandal was Harding's Watergate, and the hearts of men, at the time, were in fact merciless. He himself wasn't merciless, as Nixon often was. History has its surprises, and Nixon may survive it. But for now — inspired by Wright's poem — to feel comparable sympathy for him, I am only reminded of Heinrich Heine's witticism: "We should forgive our enemies, but only after they are hanged first."

Wright's poem is striking for its complex sympathies and the art he can muster to serve them. He does what the stronger wolf does in ritual combat: he refuses the defeated wolf's proffered jugular, the easy target. But the narrator is hardly the stronger wolf. It is Wright's achievement that, if anything, he identifies in spirit with the vulnerable Harding while employing the power of art to limn and position him for us. He stands both above his subject, and with him, and against the howling crowd.

Wright is "drunk ... in a jag for his countryman." Harding's a countryman here in a broad sense: an Ohioan, an American, a drunk, a man — as William Meredith says about a different President — just being his errors." and yet, Wright says, "he was beautiful, he was the snowfall /

Turned to white stallions standing still / Under dark elm trees." Harding *looked like* a President, and was a terribly ordinary man. Any of us who've felt a discrepancy between our inner and outer selves understands. Wright's grace, his pardoning, never denies the facts of Harding's life: "Fool," "lacks mentality," "the vaguely stunned smile." Wright's empathy is without sentimentality, though one of his great strengths as a poet is how often he dares sentimentality.

In *His Death* he balances direct and colloquial language with moments of intense lyricism. Both styles serve the poet's struggle to be equal to a man he himself feels close to on this particular evening. Wright, in addition to daring the sentimental, often approaches the precious in his attempts to register the delicate, emblematic image. When he's not as good as he can be, he descends into it. "Tonight, / the cancerous ghosts of old con men / Shed their leaves," if not precious, is at least an unfortunate mixed metaphor. But that is the poem's only lapse. The passage about Harding's beauty is gorgeous impressionism. Even so, we can take only so much of such writing. Wright's emotional timing for it is perfect in this instance, and it is wisely bookended by the straightforward "Warren lacks mentality" and the incisively direct "He died in public. He claimed the secret right / To be ashamed." The poem's aesthetic grace resides in the deft proportioning of these two dictions.

It is tempting to think that Wright's lineation in the first poem is casual, even haphazard, but given the consciously stricter formalities of the second poem we have reason to doubt that. Each line is a small or larger unit of attention, and has its own pulse—that of a man taking measure of another man, figuring out as he goes how to play the tune of him and his death. Indeed, the poem feels indebted to jazz and composition-by-field more than to the conventions of English prosody.

"Two Poems for President Harding" was included in Wright's 1963 book, *The Branch Will Not Break*, in which he found a way of speaking and moving that was in direct contradistinction to his first two traditionally metrical books. It is interesting, therefore, to see how he chose to compose the second poem, *His Tomb in Ohio*. The four consistently rhymed eight-line stanzas, and the predominantly four stress lines, metrically irregular, with the ghost of the iamb behind them, constitute a virtuoso's return to a previous method of composition. The poem demonstrates how to avoid—primarily through variation of enjambed and end-stopped lines—the narcosis of rhyme. In fact, when I've read this poem out loud to people, very few seem to recognize that it is rhymed at all. What they hear, though, are the happy, glancing clicks of cooperative sounds and, once again, the mixture of the colloquial ("I know it. But don't look at me.") and the lyrical ("Young lovers let the moon begin / Its quick spring; and the day grows old;") brought forward from the previous poem. The remarkable list of characters and their actions in the third stanza, all held and placed together by semicolons, recalls another excellent American melancholic and craftsman —Edwin Arlington Robinson. Minnegan Leonard echoes Minnever Cheevy. In both instances we suspect the names were chosen as much for their syllable count as for nominal accuracy. How do these more obvious formalities serve their subject matter? And why do we suspect that Wright employed them?

It may be, that after the first poem—essentially a riff on Harding's death and shame—Wright felt the need to honor his subject in a different, more stately way. Only the formalities are decorous, however. What Wright describes is hypocrisy and a despoiled Ohio, if not an America itself, that exists on the periphery of Harding's "ridiculous" tomb. If the first poem pardoned through empathy the fallen man, this poem dignifies its subject by contrasting him, even in his ridiculousness, to the snivelers and mockers, "the merciless," that one senses are always out there, uncomplicitous.

※

At the end of the 1993 World Series, literally after it was over, I witnessed an act that Wright's poem had prepared me to see. It's possible I wouldn't have seen it had not the poem been lodged in my consciousness. Mitch Williams, the Phillies' gifted but erratic relief pitcher, had just given up a game and Series winning home run to Toronto's Joe Carter in the bottom of the ninth. Carter, of course, was the hero, Williams the goat. The predictable jubilation occurred in the Toronto locker room, the predictable gloom in the Phillies'.

Not all reporters are merciless, and not all of the reporters gathered around Williams were merciless, but collectively, "just doing their job," they formed a merciless bunch. They wanted to know how he felt, what he was thinking, would he have thrown the same pitch had he to do it over again. If they were better men with better jobs, they would have put their arms around him, asked how they might be of help. Williams answered all of their interminable questions, made no attempt to shirk blame or to walk away. His nickname was "the wild thing" because his control on the mound was always shaky, but here he quietly and painfully endured the questions, which investigated his public failure. (Back in New Jersey, we learned later, disappointed fans were already throwing eggs at Williams' house.)

What happened next took just a few seconds, just a little longer than Jack Ruby suddenly appearing in the corner of our television screens to shoot Oswald. Except the figure we saw was Terry Mulholland, a fellow Phillies' pitcher, who reached into and through the horde of reporters to take Williams' hand, and, without saying a word, lead him away from his humiliation. Mulholland evidently could not bear what he'd been listening to, and the length of it; his act was spontaneous and arose, we suspect, from a sense of decency and from long experience with failure. Baseball players experience failure more than any other athletes. The game is so difficult that, as hitters, they're rewarded for failing more often than they succeed. A .333 batting average, for example, makes one a great hitter. It means that he fails two out of three times. Mulholland was a pitcher, and understood that he could as easily have thrown that pitch, while like Williams wishing only to do well. But Mulholland understood more: that Williams had already fulfilled his public responsibility, and that the reporters had no comparable understanding or compassion. Williams' accounting of himself was an act of fortitude. Mulholland's gesture was an act of grace.

I love that Mulholland didn't speak. It made his act God-like, a hand reaching from the heavens to offer without explanation an example to those who were ready to see it. As far as I know, no reporter wrote about it. I was moved to. I wasn't thinking of Wright's great poem when I wrote, but I've no doubt, several years later, that it exists as its significant predecessor. I present mine here to honor an act of grace. And as an homage to Wright and his poem.

GRACE

After the 1993 World Series

Mulholland extended his hand to Williams,
eased him away from the polite avidity
of reporters – good men, mostly,
just doing their jackal job for us.

Didn't we want to know exactly
what public failure felt like?
Mulholland extended his hand
because he couldn't bear what had gone

several questions too long, and Williams,
the wild thing, answering them all straight
down the middle. Mulholland must have known
but for some grace … some luck …

and how a public man is always a mistake
or two from ruin.
He extended his hand to Williams
while the rest of us watched from our safe

carpeted dens, and the Toronto players
celebrated properly in their locker room.
Back in New Jersey vandals had already thrown eggs
at Williams' house, young men no doubt

without doubt who felt others should die
for them and succeed for them and make them
happy. Oh the luxury of failing in private!
Mulholland extended his hand to Williams

who took it and walked out
of the camera's harsh eye, and into history.
Other teammates, sad themselves,
tried to console him, unsure just then –

as we were – if sympathy could reach
all the hard way to forgiveness.

Mulholland's hand reaching into the crowd comments on the crowd as it rescues from it its easy target. The hand changes nothing, except in the way that memorable acts find ways into a culture's consciousness. Williams remains the man who gave up the home run. Harding remains the failed, limited President. Mulholland's gesture and Wright's gesture, and no doubt mine, each arose out of a personal necessity, a need to enter an experience for our own sakes. The hand reaching into the crowd is crucial, but gesture and necessities are not enough to make poems. The poet must be loyal to The Three Graces.

Christianity has given us great stories of pardon and forgiveness, in other words of moral grace, but very few stories about the symmetries and felicities of art. We *are* our stories, which is why it is useful to know many. The scariest people I know are the ones who avidly subscribe to one story, one version of the world. A culture with no mythology about art is, generously put, a culture with other concerns. In America we live in such a culture, but of course have access to others. From Greek mythology we learn about The Three Graces, the three daughters of Zeus and Eurynome. Euphrosyne (joy), Thalia (bloom), and Aglaia (brilliance). They were the goddesses of the talents of music and art. Aphrodite liked them to be her companions. Young men took their oath of loyalty by them. They are represented in art as embracing each other or holding hands, clothed in flowery white garments. They stand in the foreground, for example, of Botticelli's "La Primavera."

It goes without saying that not enough people in general take their oaths of loyalty by The Three Graces. Those of us who do, artists and would-be artists, need to be careful that the oath not be too singular. We need what the goddesses represent to help us frame and elucidate the messy welter of our lives and worlds. We need to reach through and into subject matter that nags and pulses for us. To *only* give our loyalty to the principles of art is to become aesthetes.

James Wright took his oath by and to those goddesses early in his career, and increasingly learned how to betray them in ways that would still honor them. "Two Poems for President Harding," with its weavings of techniques and dictions, shows the goddesses holding hands in a way that might have impelled Botticelli to be a Cubist. The desire to be true to circumstance, both personal and historical, causes Wright to make those goddesses — as most of the 20th century has — less conventionally beautiful, less emblematic of easy harmonies. The goddesses, because they represent art, have been marvelously compliant. Joy, bloom, brilliance—we can substitute our appropriate synonyms. We know that experience becomes the forgotten past without them.

If there's such a thing as the unmediated poem—the spontaneous, lyric burst of feeling—Mulholland's gesture is its equivalent, complete in itself. My poem may reach into the crowd with Mulholland, but it does so from a greater temporal and spatial distance. We expect such a poem to measure and explore the experience it describes, though the measured poem *and* the poem-of-the-moment must in their different ways court The Three Graces. We trust that the initial courting is largely done unconsciously, suggesting not only that our best poems come from a place deeper or higher than we're aware of, but also that years of practice are behind any successful first draft. Wright's poem has the virtue of feeling both immediate and measured—his details, his images, his balancings all testify to the mysteries and skills of composition; that is, in this instance, some amalgam of grace received, grace bestowed, and grace earned.

Experience, Imagination, and the Poet as Fictionist

For the would-be poet

BROADLY SPEAKING, I ENCOUNTER TWO KINDS OF INCOMPLETE poets in my workshops, one who waits to be inspired by an event, the other for whom the act of writing is its own inspiration. The former tends to be most wedded to personal experience, the latter to language and its combinations. Both, at some point, will need to think like fictionists in order to successfully execute what they've found themselves to be doing, but the would-be poet who loves language has a considerable head start, and of the two is more likely to offer early pleasures. There are of course many other predispositions and qualities that poets need—fascination with life and its mysteries, dissatisfaction with other people's versions of it, erudition (which R.P. Blackmur defines as being intensely aware of effects), and *perseverance*, to name just a few—but for the purposes of this essay I will focus primarily on why it might be useful for poets to think of themselves as fictionists.

We begin with the knowing innocence that almost everything is available to us, that there are very few details or subjects we would *a priori* exclude. And yet we would exclude anything—even our best moment—if it did not contribute to the poem entire. Inherent in such knowledge is that our choices narrow with every word we put down, and that these constrictions are opportunities for invention and virtuosity. I find it useful to remember Marianne Moore's poem "Poetry" (her early, most anthologized version of it), with its wonderful list of what the genuine poet could make genuine. It ranged from "a wild horse taking a roll" to "business documents." Presumably all the things of this world, including "dull" things, are waiting to be vitalized by context and an interesting mind. For the poet wedded exclusively to personal experience, however, the most likely subjects are *heartbreak and how I'm feeling this very moment*, or its happier cousin *how I'm feeling this very moment*. Nothing is intrinsically wrong about those feelings or with the fact that those impulses might stir a poem. Much of the lyric tradition validates them. But for the poet inexperienced as a creator, as a shaper, the experiential poem about how or what he feels almost always leads to bad poetry.

In "Poetry," Moore says, "nor til the poets among us can be / 'literalists of / the imagination' — above insolence and triviality and can present / for inspection, 'imaginary gardens with real toads in them,' shall we have / it" [poetry]. What does she mean, and how might these claims guide poets who come to the blank page because of some heartfelt subject? Or, for that matter, poets who come with nothing specific in mind, who hope to play and intuit their way into their concerns?

In my experience with fledgling students young and old, the heartfelt subject often precludes the use of the imagination. The experience feels so large, so self-evidently what it is, that they tend to think like transcribers rather than as makers. Behind this is a second misconception, which many poets share: that others are interested in our woes and joys. They're not of course, though they may be if our language is fresh, our attitudes surprising. We need to be interested in more than ourselves. We need to enlarge our sense of what can constitute the personal so that it includes the kindred and alien experiences of our fellow humans — everything we've read about, observed, or overheard that impinges on us — not to mention our daily engagement with the less-than-visible, half-known world that we vaguely apprehend. In short, all that is not ours until we've found words to make it ours.

To be a literalist of the imagination suggests that we accurately transcribe the extra that the imagination has brought to the occasion. My guess is that *the extra* is what's already there, not easily seen or perceived. That should be our assumption about what we're seeking — not what we already know and feel, but what is not yet available, what we must write ourselves toward and into. The imagination illuminates the hard-to-see sublimities and connections that exist in the world. At all costs, we must try not to be literalists of the literal.

"Imaginary gardens," if properly created and cared for, are variously populated, and have finite boundaries. Like real gardens, they are paradigmatic of latitudes and limits, of poetry itself. As we inhabit them with our real toads or butterflies or obsessions, we are also seeking form, a shape and an outer edge that might help define what we are doing. This need not be conscious at first. Better to get lost for a while in among the colors and smells, the plenitude, and name what we see. But soon some things will deserve more importance than others. Inevitably, we will exercise our tastes and prejudices; we will begin to measure and exclude. How we give emphasis to one thing over another is both a tonal and a formal issue, and finally may be the most "personal" aspect of our poems, our most individuating act. Attention to such issues separates the artist from the amateur.

Having acknowledged all of this, I confess to desiring the heartfelt subject. It's simply what I know I must exceed and shape. The inexperienced poet tends to be overly fond of it. This prevents him / her from developing new allegiances: to unforseen language and its textures, to its rhythms and sounds, to that which the poet couldn't anticipate having said. Yet often, as we know, a news report or any "what if" impulse can be equally seminal. We know a poem can be triggered by an image, a nagging ambivalence, a rhythm — any number of small things. The task is the same with small as with large inspiration; how to exceed our original impulse, how to mingle the known with the imaginative, arrange the best words in the best order, and finally, when we've done that, to have been true to something and interesting to others.

Inexperienced poets tend not to think of themselves as fictionists. That is, as writers who must create a chain of interconnections which links the poem's occurrences, thus hinting at its purpose and design. Poet/fictionists know that their true love is the poem — that experience made of words — not the experience behind it. This may mean that as we describe the woman or man who has left us bereft, heartbroken, we're primarily interested in phrasing and pacing, not to mention the exploration of the inherent larger subject — in this case *loss* — which we must remember is not peculiar to ourselves. Maybe at the same time we're thinking of the vicissitudes of history or the quarrels among philosophers or some funky comment we heard on the street. We're ready to bring the unlikely to our subject.

The poets who first come to the page with a love for language and a desire to play with it have little trouble bringing the unlikely to their subject. Their challenge is different: to locate their real concerns as they go. When they fail it's often because their method can lead to the merely fanciful, or they, too, are inexperienced with the fictive skills that it takes to stitch together a system of cooperative details and claims. But I welcome such writers when they appear in my classes. They love their instrument. If they're serious, they might learn how to play it.

Athletes often praise a peer by saying, "He comes to play." They mean he's prepared, and gives himself wholly to his role. A classroom of would-be poets rarely hold each other to such a standard. To come to play suggests, at the least, that we've read and absorbed our betters, regularly write and revise, have begun to live with the difficulty of writing a good poem. In other words, we're ready, in Frost's phrase, to "play for mortal stakes." The less one's prepared, the lower the stakes.

For poets who play their way into seriousness there's always a moment in a poem when they face the same problem faced by other poets who've begun poems with foreknowledge of their subject. Suddenly, they know what they're doing! Their selection of details tends to become purposeful. Language loses verve. Rhythms flatten. A dulling earnestness sets in. This has happened to all of us, no matter how experienced we are. When it does, it's useful to remember how jazz musicians keep playing off of a known melody, keep *finding* the next moment while being held in and checked by everything they've already put *in the air* of their composition. They don't stop riffing; they just know a little more about their commitments. It's a time for a deepening of those commitments and/or for controlled invention. If at a comparable moment (or anytime thereafter) we surprise ourselves into still another departure, then to permit it we must adjust or tinker with our chain of causalities. Such adjustments are normal necessities for the poet as fictionist. The fictionist's credo is this: No information for information's sake. No invention for invention's sake. And no information or invention unaccompanied by other compositional virtues – an attention to phrasing, cooperative sounds, orchestration of effects. Theme or governing intention will provide further underpinning, and help keep us from making arbitrary choices. Play that remains play, which does not find some governing intention, might here and there dazzle, but at best will stir us superficially.

In his essay "Live Yak Pie," James Tate says, "What we want from poetry is to be moved, to be moved from where we now stand. We don't just want to have our ideas and emotions confirmed." It's a statement that challenges any of us who strive for emotional veracity in our poems, especially those poems that draw on personal experience. It means that no matter what we've undertaken as subject matter, part of our task is to liberate others and ourselves from stale contexts, liberate us in fact from the easily available language that confines us and limits our ability to see the world and our experience anew. And it implies that syntax might be as important as, say, insight or emotional gravity in moving us from old stances to new considerations. (In fact, it might facilitate insight and emotional gravity.) I imagine that Tate would be fond – as all poets should be – of George Oppen's definition of syntax: "A careful packing of a poem to avoid a deadening; to avoid destroying a word by its relationships."

Poems get to be poems, of course, in manifold ways. We should have nothing against the experiential or the affective, nothing against the comic or the surreal, or against any narrative tactics per se. We should feel free to employ whatever we need in order to approximate our sense of the real, which Moore would call "the genuine."

Early on in "Poetry," after offering the ploy of "I, too, dislike it," Moore says one can discover in it "a place for the genuine." She dislikes poetry, we learn, when it is "dragged into prominence by half-poets." This is a tautology, but a useful one. The genuine, presumably, is not achievable by anyone who loves, say, content more than craft, who settles for half-measures. An aspiring violinist, for example, knows what many poets don't: there are no shortcuts. Rilke wisely cautions that "the ultimate intuitions and insights will only approach one who lives in his work and remains there, and whoever considers them from afar will gain no power over them."

Too often, would-be poets believe they can tell it how it is; they confuse themselves with journalists. Poets, too, wish to tell it how it is, but have a different sense of what *it* is. Whatever *it* is, it's not immediately visible or knowable and requires all our resources, most significantly our imaginations and ability to frame and heighten effects. By the time we stop working on a poem, what may have taken weeks or months to achieve should simply seem inevitable.

Such a result is not possible for those who don't think fictively. Their tendency to value the experiential over the useful will lead to various errors of selection. If, finally, they have trouble getting out of their poems, it may be that they were never sufficiently in them, following an interior logic, conscious throughout of sonics and syntactical arrangements. They may conclude with another fact about what happened on that fateful night rather than with the crucial sonorous (or dissonant) detail that was unavailable to them before they set pen to paper.

※

Poetry and Manners

Ages with a highly developed decorum find verse a
relatively easy medium. Recent ages have clearly a
low decorum and have run toward prose.

R.P. BLACKMUR, 1951

IMAGINE WHAT BLACKMUR WOULD HAVE SAID ABOUT OUR AGE,
circa 1994. Toward what does an age run with almost no decorum?
Toward self-indulgence and the collapse of civility, he might have said.
To Hell, I would be tempted to add, which is even south of prose. But
I wonder what he might have said about verse, that now somewhat
quaint word. Would he have discovered that when there is very little
decorum a strong need for it arises, as it has in current poetry?

Even though I know that Blackmur was using "verse" to include the
greatest of poetry, I should note that these days the word suggests the
equivalent of impeccable manners and a light touch, like someone who
might be a good dinner guest, but with whom you wouldn't want to
drink late into the night. Poetry is quite another thing, criminally beau-
tiful at its best; at its least, we expect it to be surprising, idiosyncratic
perhaps, like a visitor who drops by unannounced full of compelling
news. A poem must create its own decorum, by which I mean that the
poet – through the admixture of style, content, diction, form – makes
the poem behave in ways which we as readers are persuaded that it
should behave. The poet establishes a set of proprieties that need not
be proper, but which become the poem's norms. Thus, the repetition
of "fuck" in Etheridge Knight's poem "Feeling Fucked / Up" is as nor-
mative as the recurrent use of "flew round" in Wallace Stevens' "The

Pleasure of Merely Circulating." From my standpoint, both poems be-
have rather well.

Poets sometimes write as cultural outsiders, boldly, aggressively.
They let us hear the shout, the cry; their burden, poetically speaking, is
to find a decorum even for rage. Other poets are more connected to
their particular tribe, are insiders, if you will; they act as its ears and
eyes. They aren't necessarily against anything. They are the artificers,
the makers, who *add to* the real by recording the less than visible world.
Their burden — because their voices will be quieter — is to find a deco-
rum for their poems while avoiding the merely decorous. Most poets, of
course, are some combination of outsider and insider. By registering
what it feels like to be alive and attentive to the pulses of their lives and
to the world itself, by attempting to be radically accurate, their manners
are likely to be as various as those at a dance where rival gangs with dif-
ferent tastes in music have been invited. Mostly, though, as history
shows, even outsiders consent to be graceful and balanced because they
have a stake in time-honored ways of being beautiful. Yet one need not
be conventional while obeying poetic conventions. Versifiers are those
who obey conventions without criminal intent.

My worries lately have to do with limits — both in poetry and in cul-
ture. There's been a need to correct the lack of rigor in free verse. While
I understand where this need comes from, it seems to me that the best
practitioners of free verse have always been rigorous; it's not a large con-
cern. But we do see a great deal of sloppy poetry and it exists more than
ever in a sloppy world, which seemingly has gotten crazier, out of con-
trol. I need not list the horrors. But the horrors make all of us want to
pull back, rein in. It may be why I wish for a greater civility in my small
world. If I don't know what to do, say, about how murderous our streets
have become, maybe I can effectively complain that people speak in
movie theaters while the movie is on. Pathetic, I know, the scope of my
sense of reform. Abuses which arise out of anger and deprivation are, in
many ways, more understandable to me than simple bad manners. All
of it, though, is intolerable. And this is the climate in which we write our
poems, words on paper which will correct nothing in our own time.
Outsider poems once were wilder than their historical moment, like
"Howl" in the fifties, or extravagantly resistant like "The Waste Land"

in the twenties. I'm not sure what a great outsider poem might be now. My guess is that its tenor would need to be subtler and more delicate than its historical moment, that it would be most astonishing in what it addresses yet refuses to give in to. It would surely not be the poem of outspoken complaint or rage; that poem would sound too much like the voices we regularly hear on the news. The conflation of social ills and the behavior of poems: a dangerous yoking. In an age without decorum, I need to be careful of my powerful inclination for order, if not law. I might get too much of what I desire.

Repression, as we know, can be good for language. It is often an advantage not to be able to say what we mean. We might have to resort to fable or parable, to indirection of some sort. We might have to be ingenious. For those of us who came significantly of age during the late sixties in America, repression was the dirtiest word we knew. Off with the shackles! Down with authority! Sides were clearly drawn. We knew who was right, and it wasn't them. Righteousness is certainly not very good for language. The slogan can easily start to replace the well-turned phrase. Most of us had to be wary of that. Not surprisingly in retrospect, some of the best poetry in America at this time was written by poets skilled in traditional meters and rhyme who turned to free verse. Berryman, Wright, Merwin, Kinnell, to name just a few. They had a set of noble manners from which to depart.

Meanwhile in the streets, many were finding, in the name of justice, good reasons not to be civil. As the civil rights movement itself evolved we learned not to expect angry people to be polite. Vietnam, linguistically speaking, produced passionate rhetoric and the language of confrontation, not quarrels with oneself. The sexual revolution arrived and many of us learned what beggars during The Golden Age must have observed: it wasn't happening to us. But then, amazingly, it was, or did, or could. Chivalry, thank someone, was dead, but so was courtship, which was a further blow to language; we needn't be imaginative or charming to achieve our goals. And, in concordance with all of these phenomena, the psychological community was urging people to get in touch with their feelings, as if this might be desirable. For perhaps the first time in history people went around baldly saying what they thought. On another front, Muhammed Ali, with style and humor, made public what we now call trash talking, thus invigorating the language while diminishing its value. Sportsmanship, a form of civility, was on its way out, too. Howard Cosell proved how obnoxious, yet contagious one can be by "telling it like it is." No one wanted Emily Post back, but we were developing a subterranean, growing wish for Miss Manners. A few of us needed our wrists slapped, our mouths washed out with wit. To write a sonnet at this time was at best the act of a literary Republican. And I seem to remember the word fascist being applied to a metricist once or twice.

In the early seventies, when I was teaching Marcuse and Norman O. Brown, I was fond of defining civilization to my classes as an agreement by the many to give up, for the general good, what we really wished to do. Didn't we all wish to be polymorphously perverse? The answer seemed clear. But that was when civilization seemed to be someone else's tired idea. We'd forgotten, or chose to forget, the barbarians for a while. The civilized folks were dropping the bombs, and offering rational explanations. We rallied and rallied against them. And, in private, we were sure — because it felt so self-evidently good — there was a connection between prolonged foreplay and the end of violence.

In fact we were convinced that rationality was the smokescreen of the powerful. The surreal, to many of us, seemed the only way to approximate the real. Robert Bly's impassioned "The Teeth Mother Naked at Last," in its bold associativeness and leaps of logic, was emblematic of the decorum of the time. His "Counting The Small Boned Bodies" ridiculed the euphemism "body count" by exaggerating it, and addressed the growing debasement of language. These were outsider poems that spoke intimately to the counter-culture, thus becoming insider poems for much of the poetry-reading public. Adrienne Rich, to cite another influential voice of the period, was a soul in the process of seeking her own society, which she found and helped create. Her *Diving Into The Wreck*, for example, was an outsider book that arose because she correctly saw the dominant culture, as well as the language of that culture, as antithetical to who she was and might be. We could say her book was, along with others, evidence of another kind of decorum — revisionist in its goals, direct and confrontational in its diction. While lesser poets employed the surreal as a language-game and were little more than inventively silly, and political poets less able than Rich wrote the equivalent of editorials, the best poets, as usual, remembered that in order to gain our deepest assent they had to engage us with language that went beyond wild invention and correct sentiment. (It could be argued that much of the current attenuation of free verse has its origins in the practice of surrealism without vision and right-mindedness without discovery). Few of the poems of protest had the radical decorum of, say, Berryman's *Dream Songs*, Merwin's coolly radiant enigmas in *The Lice*, or Kinnell's "The Bear" and *The Book of Nightmares*, to name just a few. Whatever source these poems came from was not immediately evident; one might say that they had surpassing manners, manners that transcended their occasions.

In the seventies, when I lived in a small town in Minnesota, I found myself more capable of generosity than ever in my life. I could *afford* to be generous. If someone needed help, I could assume that this was a singular occurrence, that similar demands on my time and emotional resources wouldn't again be made again very soon. Also, everyone in my Scandinavian-American town seemed to have a profound sense of boundaries, which meant that invitations to cross them had measurable poignancy. I suspect that people in small town America, especially in the midwest, do not feel the same loss of civility that I've been lamenting. They fear economics more than they do each other. A knock on the door is almost always neighborly. Generosity is a necessary good in sparsely populated, rural areas, and it seems that those of us in more urban environments need to recover a sense that we are dependent on one another.

At the same time I should point out — to make sure I don't romanticize small town life — that otherness is the great problem in such towns. How to survive as an *other*? The small town may be a paradigm of how boundaries can permit generosity, but it is also a place where people on the fringe, say homosexuals or intellectuals or African-Americans, develop a hunger for larger and more hospitable boundaries, those offered by cities, or, in another sense, by poems. There may be implications here for open and closed forms. That aside, true community — beyond physical parameters — often arises when you realize that everything you've thought peculiar to yourself has been thought or even lived by someone else. This is how poetry, not to mention literature in general, manifests some of its most exquisite manners; in the course of being true to itself it makes a gesture to others.

From a writer's perspective, I like what Flaubert said – I assume about the balance between repression and freedom – "Be regular and orderly in your daily life, so you can be violent and original in your work." And Donald Justice's admonition that a good poem should exhibit "that maximum amount of wildness that the form can bear" is also relevant, though again it's equally useful to think of expanding the notion of form to accommodate even more of the wild. In the last several years, the long poem and inclusiveness in general seem to be making a comeback.

I have to strain to remember the Eighties, but if a new set of manners developed then in mainstream America, it was the manners of indifference. Technology and Reaganism had much to do with this; together they were powerful determinants toward insularity and selfishness. I think of The Walkman as the symbol of the decade. A solitary person in public, on skates, listening to what no one else could hear. And I think of Reagan being called The Great Communicator and am awash in alienation, as I often was at the time, since he never communicated to me or to anyone I cared about. Oddly, perhaps not so oddly, I think it was a lively, if not good time for poetry in America. More people than ever seemed to be writing poetry, though it's not so clear that they were reading it. Still, intense pockets of interest existed throughout the country, people hungry for language and soul-work, for what technology and the marketplace couldn't provide. Their numbers were comparatively small, but I was heartened by their existence. And yet, with the exception of say, a C.K. Williams or a Louise Glück book, there was little of the anticipation that my friends and I felt in the sixties and seventies for the next collection of poems by our favorite poet. Or had I become more a captive of my prejudices and sophistication?

The New Formalism came about because free verse had lost its radical verve. Many of its practitioners had begun to misunderstand its freedoms. Its worst practitioners forgot or never knew that free verse needed to be formal, a new set of formalities for every poem. Is it merely coincidental that comparable failures of limits began to exist in the culture? On *Oprah* and *Donahue,* people speak about the awful things they did to one another in front of one another, and in front of *us.* What induces them to do this? Money? An insufficient sense of shame? It's unfair of course to liken such people to even bad free verse poets, but we can assume something similar is missing from each: the positive aspects of a compelling tradition haven't been assimilated. Nothing is making them wince. Good writers wince when they fail themselves and their craft. Good people wince when they behave badly.

At a dinner party recently, a woman — after a few drinks — asked what was wrong with her criticizing her husband's paintings in public? Didn't she have the right, she wanted to know, to express how she felt? Her husband was present in the room. I think she thought she was speaking as a feminist, and it's possible her desire to criticize his paintings was occasioned by some real and private grievance, though her style made it very difficult to be sympathetic to her. Now, in the history of boorishness this was a small thing. No doubt to all of us, at one sad time or another, have believed our private disquiets or hurts so important that they merited discomfort of others, including innocent bystanders. Or, more likely, we were simply overwhelmed, and were not "believing" anything at all; we found ourselves out of control. Such singular occurrences are almost always forgivable. The woman *did* call the next morning to apologize. It was an act of revision, a little cleaning up after a sloppy night. We welcomed it, and her. Who doesn't — in both writing and life — need second chances? Hers was an act of revision, but what would have been more difficult, and therefore more praiseworthy, would have been an act of grace — a seldom used word for obvious reasons.

While she was criticizing her husband's paintings, I kept thinking of Frost's wonderful line, "We shall be known by the delicacy of where we stop short." I've also thought of that line at countless poetry readings where the poets — without the felicities of language or form — told me more than I could possibly want to know about their private lives. In a culture with little or no decorum, and a comparable lack of personal responsibility, sometimes what we choose not to do may be how we will be best known. It certainly will be a hallmark of grace. Too often, as William Meredith reminds us in a poem, we consent to be our worst selves whether we're drunk or not.

Is civility, if not grace, always what people in power have a vested interest in maintaining? What stake, if any, do or should the powerless have in civility? And is this relevant at all to the world of poetry and poets? Blackmur once said of Wallace Stevens: "... erudite, by which I mean intensely careful of effects." I would like to think that the angry, the disenfranchised, would wish to be intensely careful of effects, though in ways perhaps that are ruder than those in power might like. But that's probably my wishful thinking. The disenfranchised, acting individually, often just want to break down the door, regardless of the consequences. They don't want to be criminally beautiful, nor do they want to be particularly efficacious. As writers, whether we're outsiders or insiders, we try to control how our words behave in conjunction with one another, or we allow them their legendary promiscuity. In the case of protesters, revolt is either in the control of people profoundly erudite (in Blackmur's definition), or the merely furious will act alone and cause havoc, and not be useful to the cause. Successful rebellion and successful poetry writing are finally the provinces of experts, who learn as they go. Rebellion and poetry writing may begin in grief and rancor, but they must be brought to conclusion by passionate tacticians. Coleridge's notion of poetry as something with "more than usual emotion and more than usual order" may apply here. The civility I want in the culture is fraught with the fact that people are even more unruly than words, sometimes for good reason, and that I believe in democracy and its annoyances. I, of course, don't believe in democracy when it comes to poetry. Poets try to exercise a sweet tyranny over their words. That their words often seem willful is one of the difficulties, and, I should add, pleasures of composition. On the other hand, the willfulness of have-nots, and of competing claimants for fairness and justice, increasingly suggest the irreconcilability of inequality and anyone's vain desire for an orderly life. I acknowledge this and acknowledge at the same time that most of the culture, only part of which includes people with legitimate gripes, has become murderous, shameless, insensitive to language and the daily lives of others.

It's the small things that irk me most, probably because they're the most likely to repeat themselves. The salesman on the phone addressing you by your first name, the sullen clerk responding with a shrug.

Which is why it seems to me there are more opportunities for grace than ever before. I love James Wright, for example, who knew that "the hearts of men are merciless" and therefore was able in a poem not to vilify or caricaturize, but in fact sympathize with President Harding, that easy target. And I love the kindnesses of people who have no reason to be kind to you, but are. Such kindnesses happen every day amid all the other occasions for despair. Once we would have called them normal kindnesses, but when they occur in a climate in which fear and self-protectedness are daily givens, they are noteworthy. If I said earlier that we shall be known by the delicacy of where we stop short, I would like — without invalidating that sentiment — to amend it. We shall be known by our uncommon gestures, our surpassing gestures. Perhaps here is where poetry and manners most truly converge. Both, at their highest levels, involve doing gracefully what is *not* expected of us.

Love's Artifice and Fernando Pessoa

WE DON'T EXPECT LOVE POEMS WRITTEN IN THE INITIAL STAGES OF love to be very complicated. They tend to extol the beloved, or celebrate love itself. We can be pretty sure they won't have a "but" in them. They are poems of the heightened moment, often exuberant, sometimes hyperbolic. If their authors have other attitudes about love, those attitudes are temporarily subsumed by feelings that do not call themselves into question. Better that these authors be young; their task is simpler. A good, unabashed love poem by someone of age and experience is another kind of achievement. At the very least, it's a triumph over history, often one's own.

Discrimination, perspective — the very qualities we require from poems of experience — tend not to be brought to poems-of-the-moment. Presumably, they're happily unavailable, the poet awash in emotions that instead lead to other virtues: immediacy and elan. Yet it would be naive of us to think that such a poet isn't making choices as the poem evolves. The act of writing a (good) poem involves selection and usually some consciousness of artifice, even when one seems wildly carried away. And we trust that before long the hot, ardent poem will in the revision process get the cool eye. It's often a cool eye that decides to keep immediacy immediate. More often than not the authors of love poems have some distance from their real-life situations, or from love in general. The states of mind that are inimical to loving — having a strategy, a desire to develop new allegiances — are often the postures that make love poems work. In the act of writing, the poet must value the poem more than the beloved.

Fernando Pessoa, the Portuguese poet and writer, wrote under his own name and under three heteronyms. Alvaro de Campos and Ricardo Reis mostly wrote in prose, often arguing with each other over aesthetic differences. Alberto Caiero, his major heteronym, was an unschooled shepherd poet of total sense-feeling. Pessoa invested each with a distinct style and personality. He believed that 'to pretend is to know oneself,' and it is his thinking on the lyric that I will examine here, especially as it relates to one manifestation of the lyric impulse, the love poem and its varieties. While not discussing love poems per se, Pessoa makes bold claims about emotion and depersonalization, which persuade and also raise questions. Just how much distance from subject and self is useful? On what contextual issues will it depend?

In his book of Selected Prose *Always Astonished*, edited by Edwin Honig (from whom I've borrowed much of the information in the above paragraph), Pessoa states with characteristic authority,

> Three sorts of emotions produce great poetry – strong but
> quick emotions, seized upon for art as soon as they have
> passed, *but not before they have passed* (italics mine);
> strong and deep emotions in their remembrance a long
> time after; and false emotions, that is to say, emotions felt
> in the intellect. Not insincerity, yet a translated sincerity, is
> the basis of all art.

Pessoa goes on to refine these notions in a chapter called "The Manipulation of Sensibility" in which he makes distinctions about the levels of lyric poetry. The first level is suggestive of the purely celebrational lyric, which he devalues.

> The first level of lyric poetry is that in which the poet, of
> an intensely emotive temperament, expresses sponta-
> neously or reflectively that temperament and those emo-
> tions. It is the most common type of lyric poet; also, it is
> the the least estimable, as a type. The intensity of emotion
> proceeds, in general, from the unity of temperament, so
> this type of lyric poet is generally monotonic, and his poems
> revolve around a fixed, usually small number of emotions.

We recognize this as astute, if not definitive. Two famous poems of our tradition come to mind – Shakespeare's "Let me not to the marriage of true minds / admit impediments" and Robert Burns' "A Red, Red Rose" — as examples of the first-level lyric. Shakespeare's sonnet proffers, and goes on to make an argument that true love doesn't change over time. Almost everyone who has loved knows that Shakespeare is wrong, but wrong in the way that we allow lovers to be wrong; we must honor their delusions, if for no other reason than we've known them to be our own. The sonnet is admirable for the ingenuity of its conceit and its deft phrasing. But it is monotonic. It places no impediment in the way of either its thinking or its feeling. Similarly, Burns begins his poem with "O my Luve's like a red, red rose, / That's newly sprung in June" and extols the beloved all the way through. The poem doesn't aspire to complexity of feeling, but to song, and its pleasures are in fact musical. It establishes and satisfies its own terms. Within its one emotional note, Burns has borrowed from various Scottish folk songs and stitched together a paean to his love. Unlike Shakespeare, he doesn't attempt to make an argument, and we feel no inclination to quarrel with the poem. But for what it's worth, we sense what Pessoa was talking about.

By degree, Elizabeth Barrett Browning's sonnet that begins "How do I love thee, let me count the ways," while remaining a first-level lyric, is reflective, suggestive of a love of some duration, and of a mind seeking emotional precision. The poet does more than assert her love, she measures it against lost verities. Throughout there's an implication that she has examined as well as lived her love life. Lines like "I love thee to the level of everyday's / most quiet need" and "I love thee purely, as men turn from praise" are evidence of a quality of mind and achieved phrasing that make her declarations of love attractive for us to overhear. But "I love thee with the breath, / Smiles, tears of all my life" and "...if God choose, / I shall but love thee better after death" are unfortunate, close to Hallmark moments, and certainly keep this poem from being considered great poetry. Nevertheless, Browning's love poem, while arguably monotonic, suggests another level of a level-one lyric: the wholly affirmative love poem written as meditation, thus from a greater distance. At its best, it shows some of the virtues of emotions recollected in tranquility. It acknowledges old griefs, a disconnection from beauty and grace, lost saints. It is a song of experience.

These are poems we'd like to find on our pillows, or receive in the mail. They *do* "revolve about a fixed, usually small number of emo-tions," yet are not without artifice. Their details are merely governed by one mode of selection, of which the writer is aware. No failure here. Each poem has lived up to its intentions. It's exactly those intentions that Pessoa has chosen to evaluate. His second level of lyric poetry is that

> in which the poet, being more intellectual or imaginative
> or even simply more cultured, no longer has the simplicity
> of emotions or their limitations that distinguish the poet
> on the first level. He will also be typically a lyric poet in the
> general sense of the term but will not be a monotonic poet.

A poem that perhaps bridges the first and second levels is "Magic Spell of Rain" by Rumanian poet Ana Blandiana, translated by Chrisula Stefanescu & Inta Moriss-Wiest.

MAGIC SPELL OF RAIN

I love the rain, I passionately love the rain,
the mad rains and the gentle rains,
the chaste rains and the rains like unbridled women,
refreshing rains and endless, boring rains.
I love the rain, I passionately love the rain.
I like to wallow in its tall white grass,
I like to break its threads and walk with them in my teeth
so that men watching me grow dizzy.
I know it isn't nice to say, *I am the most beautiful woman on earth*,
it isn't nice and maybe isn't even true,
but allow me, when it rains,
only when it rains,
to say the magic words, *I am the most beautiful woman on earth*,
the most beautiful, because it is raining,
and the fringes of rain in my hair become me.
I am the most beautiful woman because the wind blows
and my dress desperately struggles to hide my knees.
I am the most beautiful woman because you
are far away, and I am waiting for you,
and you know I am waiting.
I am the most beautiful woman because I know how to wait,
and still I wait.
There's an intense scent of love in the air.

> People passing by sniff the rain to catch its traces.
> In such a rain, one can fall in love in an instant.
> All those who pass by are in love
> and I am waiting for you.
> I love the rain,
> I passionately love the rain,
> the mad rains and the gentle rains,
> the chaste rains and the rains like unbridled women.

The poem is a celebration of being in love, and makes use of the relative freedoms of free verse to find rhythms and language equal to its author's high spirits. Blandiana's primary technical device is recurrence. "Rain" is her prop and motif. Although the poem is purportedly addressed to the beloved, we don't learn this until near the end. This is useful because it allows us for a while to believe the poem is addressed to us, so when Blandiana says "I am the most beautiful woman on earth" and then offers her wry self-conscious disclaimers, we can entertain that she's asking for our forbearance. "I know it isn't nice to say" and "maybe it isn't even true" are winks to the reader that say, in effect, "This is how I get you to accept the unacceptable. I am a woman in love and this is how I feel, and you will forgive me." We also allow Blandiana to say what she says because she's signalled from the beginning that her poem is going to proceed extravagantly. She likes to wallow in the rain's tall white grass, she likes to break its threads and walk with them in her teeth. This is a poet riding her eros toward and into language that will equal and embody it. By mid-poem, we are attuned not only to the poem's extravagances, but to the fact that we're in the presence of an orchestration of extravagances. In this sense, "Magic Spell of Rain" is more fictive than the poems previously discussed, simultaneously wooing the reader and the beloved. Its details feel like gestures, its pacing and music constitute an arrangement, albeit emotionally based. And it isn't monotonic. A tonal playfulness reigns for two-thirds of the poem and then gives way to what is tempting to call a lover's sincerity, heralded by the "I am waiting for you" repetitions. This is where the addressee of the poem is revealed and the poem turns and deepens. The revelation of "I am waiting for you" feels like artful sincerity, both felt and well-timed.

Can we also call it a "translated sincerity," which Pessoa claims is the basis for all art? If a translated sincerity means taking a "false" emotion, one not authentically felt, and converting it by imagination and empathetic intelligence into one that feels authentic, no, I don't think his term applies here. There's more of a strategical, compositional matter involved. How to construct a poem that will arrange and control the order of its disclosures. By poem's end, it's clear that Blandiana's allegiances to language, rhythm, and structure were equal (if not more so) to any allegiances she had to subject matter at the poem's outset. We sense that the poem's selection process, perhaps initially governed by the brio of being in love, found a few more things to be true to. The poet found herself alternately exuberant, bemused, sincere, until the entire poem became a conflation of those feelings.

Yehuda Amichai's "Gifts of Love," (tr. by Stephen Mitchell & Chana Bloch) seems to fall wholly within Pessoa's multi-toned second level, and engagingly blurs the sincerity / insincerity question.

GIFTS OF LOVE

I gave them to you
for your clothes, your fingers. I gilded
the time on your wrist,
I hung a lot of glittery things on you
so you'd sway for me in the wind, so you'd
chime softly over me
to soothe my sleep.

I comforted you with apples, as it says
in the Song of Songs,
I lined your bed with them,
so we could roll smoothly on red apple-bearings.

I covered your skin with a pink chiffon,
transparent as baby lizards – the ones with
black diamond eyes on summer nights.

You helped me to live for a couple of months
without needing religion
or a point of view.

> You gave me a letter opener of silver.
> Real letters aren't opened that way;
> they're torn open,
> torn, *torn.*

We're quite sure that the things the poet claims to have done for his beloved are so stylized as to be somewhere in between the actual and the fabulous. He may have given her earrings and rings, as the first few lines suggest, but after that we feel in the presence of an imagination that's sly and deliberately hyperbolic. "I covered you with apples..." is so — if not insincere — at least literary (borrowed from "The Song of Songs"), that we have an enactment of what might constitute "a translated sincerity." We know we're involved with a fictionist, someone whose gestures are designed to serve the heightened occasion *and* to enchant.

When a stanza later we overhear the apparently straight "You helped me to live for a couple of months / without needing religion / or a point of view," we feel the "cultural" sophistication, as Pessoa might call it, of a poet who has enough distance and savvy to abstract and measure the way love releases one from familiar preoccupations. This makes the ending even more of a turn, and more brilliant. The self-consciousness we've just witnessed is replaced by passion. The beloved has made a mistake, offered the gift that is, we trust, well-meant, but emblematic of an intolerable gentility and cooler emotions. The lover asserts that real letters (passionate love letters?) will be torn open, *torn.* No silver letter openers for him. This is the poem's final artifice. We are as pleased by the speed of the move as we are by its content. Both are synechdochic of why this love poem is written in the past tense.

Sue Ellen Thompson's "How To Tell a True Love Story" falls somewhere in between Pessoa's second and third levels. It declares itself as a fiction, maybe a metafiction. The title suggests that a depersonalized poem will follow, and it will for a while, but only for a while.

HOW TO TELL A TRUE LOVE STORY

> Always begin with the light, how it lay
> like a tarnish upon the glass

beyond which rose the ancient walls
of the city that might have been theirs.

Say he pulled her face roughly to his,
the way he once grasped a coconut

on the black sand beach, pausing to take
its sweetness in first through the eyes;

or say he pulled her down like a rare book,
his face dissolving in wonder

as he fingered the leaves of her smile. We will bring
our own urgencies to the scene.

Put some obstacle in the way of their lovemaking:
have her wearing those tapered jeans

he must pick at her heels to remove; or let
their bodies impede, his elbow snagging

a silken breast, her teeth meeting his in a kiss
that clacks like bone. Let them fail

to get it right, so there will be something unfinished
between them, something that blights

the small green fruit of their meeting
and fades into correspondence. And let

their correspondence drop off, a misunderstanding,
a failure of passion or nerve. But end

where love as I would have you tell it
ends, when he opens the door

to the retreating light and she falls
through the unnamed space between this moment

and the next without seeing where she is going,
or who it is that trembles there above her.

Pessoa's definition of the third level of lyric poetry is this:

> in which the poet, more intellectual still, begins to deper-
> sonalize, not just because he feels, but because he thinks
> he feels — feels states of the soul that he really does not
> possess, simply because he understands them. We are on
> the threshold of dramatic poetry in its innermost essence.
> The temperament of the poet, be that as it may, is dis-
> solved by the intelligence.

Well, something like this almost happens in "How to Tell…" Be-
cause it announces that it has a strategy, we prepare ourselves to listen
for that strategy as we are told the story itself. Artifice is not disguised.
The poem presents a provisional scene, to which Thompson trusts
"we'll bring our own urgencies." The poet knows that obstacles are op-
portunities. She suggests that if it were our poem, we should place some
in our way. And we sense that she knows love scenes are funny, at least
those that are self-consciously observed. The line break after "fail," art-
fully and comically raises one possibility, which the next line cancels
and refines. Certainly from the outset the word "True" in the title has
haunted the poem. What is a "true" love poem, according to Thomp-
son? Perhaps a poem that knows all the precarious and funny condi-
tions of love, demonstrates its sophistication about such conditions, yet
also is able to acknowledge love's mystery and awe. Irony gives way to
poignancy in the the last three couplets. Such, we trust, is the drift of
love altered or accentuated by passion. The scene diffuses into a kind of
lover's haze, the man and (especially) the woman no longer certain of
what is happening to them. Still, even at this moment, we're aware that
an authorial strategy has been enacted, and that the final touch of this
strategy is to transcend the comic.

"How To Tell A True Love Story" comes somewhat close to Pessoa's
lyric ideal because Thompson not only understands "the states of the
soul" she evinces, but seems to feel them as well. "How To Tell… ,"
though, seems to only partially testify "to a temperament dissolved by
the intelligence." Rather than dissolved, I sense a temperament actual-
ized by intelligence. I admire what I sense, but I'm much too aware
of the poet's moves to think that the poet's temperament has been

dissolved. This poem, like many others, won't fit neatly into Pessoa's categories. In fact, its conspicuous artifice is part of the poem's virtues. We're supposed to see its elbows. When the "I" appears late in the poem, it personalizes the poem, rescuing it from depersonalization.

Pessoa cites Robert Browning and Tennyson as practicioners of the third level lyric, arguing that when "the temperament of the poet is…dissolved by the intelligence…we are on the verge of dramatic poetry." In his fourth (and final) level he uses Shakespeare as an example of someone "who not only feels but lives in states of soul he does not possess directly," and thus fully undergoes a kind of depersonalization that permits him to be everyone. Convincingly and seamlessly. Clearly, he is talking about Shakespeare the playwright. He appropriately mentions Robert Browning as belonging on this level as well. We can see why Pessoa with his many personae would have been interested in work that aspires to such depersonalization. But he is wise enough not to be an absolutist on the subject. He suggests that the lyric poet advance "one rung up the ladder of depersonalization," not necessarily all the way to dramatic poetry.

I would recommend that we lyric poets follow his wisdom only as far as distancing ourselves from our subject matter serves to enhance that subject matter. Just how far is a conditional issue, finally to be determined by our temperaments, aesthetic predispositions, and most particularly, by the practical contextual imperatives of each poem we write. It is easy to imagine depersonalization serving certain subjects (sensational subjects, for example, and not serving others (some love poems), though we can imagine degrees of depersonalization serving most poems. Maybe achieving maximum closeness to our subjects while still being able to manage our effects is what's most desirable, and perhaps not antithetical to Pessoa's precepts.

John Logan's "Suzanne" is evocative of such a managed closeness.

SUZANNE

You make us want to stay alive, Suzanne,
the way you turn

your blonde head.
The way you curve your slim hand

toward your breast.
When you drew your legs

up, sitting by the fire,
and let your bronze hair

stream about your knees
I could see the grief

of the girl in your eyes.
It touched the high,

formal bones of your face.
Once I heard it in your lovely voice

when you sang —
the terrible time of being young.

Yet you bring us joy with your
self, Suzanne, wherever you are.

And, once, although I wasn't here,
you left three roses on my stair.

One party night when you were high
you fled barefoot down the hall,

the fountain of your laughter
showering through the air.

"Chartreuse," you chanted
(the liqueur you always wanted),

"I have yellow chartreuse hair!"
Oh it was a great affair.

You were the most exciting person there.
Yesterday when I wasn't here

again,
you brought a blue, porcelain

egg to me —
colored beautifully

for the Russian Easter.
Since then, I have wanted to be your lover,

but I have only touched your shoulder
and let my fingers brush your hair,

because you left three roses on my stair.

In this intimate address to Suzanne, this paean to her virtues, Logan (or, if you will, his persona) acknowledges his desire for her but does not insist on it. If it is a seduction poem, it attempts to seduce by sentiment via song, not by overt persuasion. The addressee is neither coy mistress nor ardent pursuer. She behaves as he does, fondly but somewhat cautiously. She leaves things for him when he's not present; he's presumably writing rather than speaking to her in person. While these moves are engaging, they are not the poem's major pleasures.

Logan is at least as interested in enchanting us with the poem's music as he is in writing an efficacious love poem. After four or five couplets, we can be sure that this is true. He manages the flow and feel of sentiment with deft near rhymes, then with exact rhymes, and all along with assonance and consonance — felicities that we come to anticipate and welcome. Logan, in fact, was one of our great casual rhymers; his balance of enjambed and end-stopped lines almost always modulate the recurrence of similar sounds *and* help maintain a feel of natural speech. His artifice is conspicuous. But at the same time it's winking at us. We tend not to accuse winkers of the "crime" they are committing.

The poem's only overt distancing device occurs immediately. "You make *us* [italics mine] want to stay alive, Suzanne," And again fifteen lines later, "Yet you bring us joy with your / self, Suzanne, wherever you are." (Logan never indicates who the "us" is, which is perhaps one of the latitudes of the lyric poet.) The suggestion is twofold: that Suzanne is broadly appealing, and that the poet has not spent time with her in private. His stance, though adoring, is reticent, as evidenced by the verb tense in "Since then I have wanted to be your lover." He is the kind of would-be lover, we imagine, who might succeed in the manner that some good poems do with their readers; enough room has been left for the addressee to voluntarily bring herself to the occasion. She has not been cajoled, except in the way a suitor standing below a balcony with a guitar cajoles. All those final r sounds are as risky as they are irresistible, and show Logan's aural virtuosity.. "Aesthetic intimacy," William Matthews once called this kind of achievement.

A simple feeler and emoter could not have written "Suzanne." Even though the "I" in the poem is probably not far removed from who the author is, I suspect that Pessoa would have felt that Logan, as maker, was nevertheless a few rungs up the desirable ladder.

I've just speculated that, in love poems, it's desirable for authors to achieve maximum closeness to subject while maintaining enough distance to orchestrate their effects. I would add that this is especially desirable if the love poem is addressed to the beloved. But perhaps the poem that's interested in love per se requires a different strategy, a different authorial stance. Irony, of course, is one of the ways in which we distance ourselves from experience. In our lives (in the short run, at least), it allows us to manage the situation. One would think it a hindrance to intimacy and no doubt when overused it is. But a fictionist, a Pessoa perhaps, might insist that it depends on context and the adroitness of the artist. A lover might claim that irony at a cocktail party got him to the bedroom and maybe to the altar where he was then happy to discard it. We would need to feel sure about his tone and overall intent in order to judge him. Thompson's "How To Tell A True Love Story" proves that irony can even facilitate intimacy if irony is abandoned at just the right time. But an ironist can never fall into Pessoa's first level category. That fact might constitute his sadness as well as his strength. John Barth's protagonist says at the end of "Lost In The Funhouse" that he'd rather be the lover for whom funhouses are built. e.e. cummings wrote that "he who pays attention to the syntax of things / will never wholly kiss you." Alas, the builder always has some distance. The trick sometimes is to forget we're builders and ride some élan or wildness for as long as we can. Most of us can't help but be builders anyway.

One way of thinking of Pessoa's dicta is to know that finally our major allegiance must switch from self and experience to the poem entire. That's the real art of depersonalization. There are many ways to achieve it.

I'll offer one final, ironic example, Wislawa Szymborska's "True Love" (translated by Stanislaw Baranczak and Clare Cavanaugh).

TRUE LOVE

True love. Is it normal,
is it serious, is it practical?
What does the world get from two people
who exist in a world of their own?

Placed on the same pedestal for no good reason,
drawn randomly from millions, but convinced
it had to happen this way — in reward for what?
     For nothing.
The light descends from nowhere.
Why on these two and not on others?
Doesn't this outrage justice? Yes it does.
Doesn't it disrupt our painstakingly erected principles,
and cast the moral from the peak? Yes on both accounts.

Look at the happy couple.
Couldn't they at least try to hide it,
fake a little depression for their friends' sake!
Listen to them laughing — it's an insult.
The language they use — deceptively clear.
And their little celebrations, rituals,
the elaborate mutual routines —
it's obviously a plot behind the human race's back!

It's hard even to guess how far things might go
if people start to follow their example.
What could religion and poetry count on?
What would be remembered? What renounced?

True love. Is it necessary?
Tact and common sense tell us to pass over it in silence,

like a scandal in Life's highest circles.
Perfectly good children are born without its help.
It couldn't populate the planet in a million years,
it comes along so rarely.

Let the people who never find true love
keep saying that there's no such thing.

Their faith will make it easier for them to live and die.

Her strategy permits her several virtues, intelligence and humor chief among them. But the poem's final and most pleasing achievement is its discrediting of cynicism and simultaneously its elevation of "true love." Clearly, for a long while, we enjoy the cynicism of the speaker, even while we suspect that it's an authorial strategy. Everything the speaker says and rhetorically questions has the accuracy of a person with a telescope commenting on a circus show down the road. The comments are often funny in their socio-scientific manner, and we are gradually made aware that Szymborska's mock utilitarian speaker has never been smitten out of her intelligence. Szymborska doesn't alter the poem's distance to effect the change in stance, as Sue Ellen Thompson does at the end of "How To Tell a True Love Story." She keeps an ironic posture until the end. "Let the people who never find true love / keep saying that there's no such thing. Their faith will make it easier for them to live and die." The difference is that the irony now is turned against the poem and its argument, casting another light on it and deepening it. We can say here that distance has served intimacy, and that the poet has disappeared into her subject in a way that Pessoa would admire. Maybe this is most possible in poems that wish to explore love as opposed to asserting it. In love poems intended to extol the beloved, the "I" is necessarily less tricky, its assertions less subject to examination and interpretation. This is why Pessoa's hierarchies of the lyric finally persuade more than they beg questions. The advanced levels of the lyric, by degree subsuming the I to the subject at hand, invite both poet and audience to bring more attitudes to the occasion.

ACKNOWLEDGMENTS

Akhmatova, Anna: "Summer Garden" from *You Will Hear Thunder: Anna Akhmatova Selected Poems*, translated by D.M. Thomas, published by Martin Secker & Warburg. Reprinted by permission of The Random House Group Ltd.

Amichai, Yehuda: "Gifts of Love," from *The Selected Poetry of Yehuda Amichai*, translated/edited by Chana Bloch and Stephen Mitchell, copyright © 1996 by The Regents of the University of California. Reprinted with the permission of the University of California Press.

Berry, Wendell: "Marriage," © 1967. Reprinted with the permission of The Spieler Agency West.

Booth, Philip: "Saying It," from *Relations: New and Selected Poems* by Philip Booth, copyright © 1986 by Philip Booth. Used by permission of Viking Penguin, a division of Penguin Putnam, Inc.

Carpenter, William: "Rain" from *Rain*, copyright 1985. Reprinted with the permission of the author.

Celan, Paul: "Fugue of Death," translated by Christopher Middleton. Reprinted with the permission of Christopher Middleton.

de Andrade, Carlos: "Your Shoulders Hold up the World," from *Traveling in the Family: Selected Poems* by Carlos Drummond de Andrade. Copyright © 1986 by Carlos de Andrade and Thomas Colchie. Reprinted by permission of Random House, Inc.

Heaney, Seamus: "Punishment" from *Poems 1965–1975* by Seamus Heaney. Copyright © 1980 by Seamus Heaney. Reprinted by permission of Farrar, Straus and Giroux, LLC.

Hughes, Ted: "Crow Blacker Than Ever," from *Crow*, by Ted Hughes, reprinted by permission of Faber and Faber Ltd.

Jarrell, Randall, "Next Day," and "Protocols," from *The Complete Poems*, by Randall Jarrell. Copyright © 1969, renewed 1997 Mary von S. Jarrell.

Kafka, Franz: Excerpt from "The Silence of the Sirens," from *Franz Kafka: The Complete Stories*, copyright © 1971 by Schoken Books. Reprinted with the permission of Schoken Books, a division of Random House, Inc.

Larkin, Philip: Excerpt from "Church Going" from *Collected Poems* by Philip Larkin. Copyright © 1988, 1989 by the Estate of Philip Larkin. Reprinted by permission of Farrar, Straus and Giroux, LLC.

McCarriston, Linda: "Healing the Mare," from *Eva-Mary*, Tri-Quarterly Books, copyright 1991. Reprinted with the permission of the author.

Meredith, William: "A Mild-Spoken Citizen Finally Writes to the White House" and "Crossing Over" are reprinted from *Effort at Speech: New and Selected Poems* by William Meredith, published by TriQuarterly Books / Northwestern University Press in 1997. Copyright © 1997 by William Meredith. All rights reserved; used by permission of Northwestern University Press and the author.

Merwin, W.S.: "For the Anniversary of My Death," © 1963, 1964, 1965, 1966, 1967 by W.S. Merwin, used by permission of The Wylie Agency, Inc.

Piercy, Marge, "The Friend," from *Circles on the Water*, copyright 1982 by Alfred A. Knopf, published by Alfred A. Knopf. Reprinted with the permission of the author.

Popa, Vasko: "Prudent Triangle," translated by Charles Simic. Reprinted with the permission of Charles Simic.

Rich, Adrienne: The Lines from "Diving into the Wreck," from *Diving Into the Wreck: Poems 1971–1972* by Adrienne Rich. Copyright © 1973 by W. W. Norton & Company, Inc. Used by permission of the author and W. W. Norton & Company, Inc.

Roethke, Theodore: "Dolor," copyright 1943 by Modern Poetry Association, inc., from *Collected Poems of Theodore Roethke* by Theodore Roethke. Used by permission of Doubleday, a division of Random House.

Schott, Penelope: "Men Can Leave," from *These Are My Same Hands*, State Street Press, 1989.

Snyder, Gary: "How Poetry Comes to Me," from *No Nature: New and Selected Poems* by Gary Snyder. Copyright © 1992 by Gary Snyder. Reprinted by permission of Random House, Inc.

Stafford, William: "The Little Ways That Encourage Good Fortune" copyright 1973, 1998 by the Estate of William Stafford. Reprinted from *The Way It Is: New & Selected Poems* with the permission of Graywolf Press, Saint Paul, Minnesota.

Stevens, Wallace: Excerpt from "The Idea of Order at Key West," from *Collected Poems* by Wallace Stevens. Copyright 1936 by Wallace Stevens and renewed 1964 by Holly Stevens. Reprinted by permission of Alfred A. Knopf, a division of Random House, Inc.

Szymborska, Wislawa: "True Love" from *View with a Grain of Sand*, copyright © 1993 by Wislawa Szymborska, English translation by Stanislaw Baranczak and Clare Cavanagh copyright © 1995 by Harcourt, Inc., reprinted by permission of the publisher.

Thompson, Sue Ellen: "How to Tell a True Love Story," copyright 1995, published by Owl Creek Press. Reprinted from *The Wedding Boat* with the permission of the publisher and the author.

Voigt, Ellen Bryant: "Dancing With Poets," from *The Lotus Flowers* by Ellen Bryant Voigt. Copyright © 1987 by Ellen Bryant Voigt. Used by permission of W. W. Norton & Company, Inc.

von Goethe, Johann Wofgang: "The Holy Longing," translated by Robert Bly, from *News of the Universe: Poems of Twofold Consciousness*, edited by Robert Bly. Copyright © 1980, 1995 by Robert Bly. Reprinted with the permission of Sierra Club Books.

Williams, C.K. "Gas Station," from *Selected Poems* by C.K. Williams. Copyright © 1994 by C.K. Williams. Reprinted by permission of Farrar, Straus and Giroux, LLC.

Wright, Charles: Excerpt from "Disjecta Memmbra" from *Black Zodiac* by Charles Wright. Copyright © 1997 by Charles Wright. Reprinted by permission of Farrar, Straus and Giroux, LLC.

ABOUT THE AUTHOR

Stephen Dunn is the author of eleven collections of poetry, including the recent *Different Hours* (W.W. Norton & Co.), and *Loosestrife* (W.W. Norton & Co.), a National Book Critics Circle finalist in 1996. He received an Academy Award in Literature from The American Academy of Arts and Letters in 1995. Among his other awards are the Levinson Prize from *Poetry*, and fellowships from the Rockefeller and Guggenheim Foundations. He is a Trustee Fellow in the Arts at Richard Stockton College of New Jersey.

INDEX

The publication of this book was made possible,
in part, by the special support of the following individuals:

Dane & Judy Gordon,
Richard Garth & Mimi Hwang,
Tom & Peggy Hubbard, Peter & Robin Hursh,
Robert & Willy Hursh, Archie & Pat Kutz,
Jennifer & Craig Litt, Timothy Madigan, Peter & Phyllis Makuck,
Boo Poulin, Robert B. Shea, Allen & Suzy Spencer,
Judith Taylor, Robert & Lee Ward,
Pat & Michael Wilder

✛

Cover Design is by Lisa Mauro / Mauro Design, Rochester, New York

Art: *Pure Interval* (oil on paper) by Steve Carpenter, Courtesy of the Artist

Interior design by Valerie Brewster, Scribe Typography,
Port Townsend Washington. The type is Bulmer, designed by
William Martin in the late 18th century.

Manufacturing was by McNaughton & Gunn,
Saline, Michigan.